Jacobean Rhapsodies

Composing with 28 Appliqué Designs

Patricia B. Campbell & Mimi Ayars

C&T PUBLISHING

Copyright © 1998 Patricia B. Campbell and Mimi Ayars

Developmental Editor: Barbara Konzak Kuhn
Technical Editor: Sally Loss Lanzarotti
Book Design: John Cram
Cover Design: Kathy Lee; Design 16 is shown on the cover.
Illustrator: Richard Sheppard © C&T Publishing, Inc.

All photography by Michael Bodycomb, Ft. Worth, TX
unless otherwise noted.

Attention Teachers:
C&T Publishing, Inc. encourages you to use this book as a
text for teaching. Contact us at 800-284-1114 or
www.ctpub.com for more information about the C&T
Teachers Program.

Library of Congress Cataloging-in-Publication Data
Campbell, Patricia B.
    Jacobean rhapsodies: composing with 28 appliqué
designs / Patricia B. Campbell and Mimi Ayars.
        p. cm.
    Includes bibliographical references and index.
    ISBN 1-57120-049-5
        1. Appliqué—Patterns. 2. Quilting—Patterns.
3. Decoration and ornament, Jacobean. I. Ayars, Mimi.
II. Title.
TT779.C365   1998
746.46'041—dc21   98-6691
                                              CIP

Berol Prismacolor Pencil is a registered trademark of
    Empire Berol U.S.A.
Celtic Bias Bar is a registered trademark of Celtic Design
    Company.
Clover needles are a registered trademark of Clover Mfg.
    Co., Ltd.
Fasturn is a registered trademark of Crowning Touch, Inc.
Fiskars is a registered trademark of Fiskars, Inc.
Gingher is a registered trademark of Gingher, Inc.
Ott-Light is a registered trademark of Environmental
    Design Concepts.
Pentel Clic is a trademark of Pentel Company, LTC.
Pigma Micron is a registered trademark of Sakura.
Poly-Down is a registered trademark of Hobbs Bonded
    Fibers.
Sharpie is a registered trademark of Sanford Corporation.
Simplicity is a registered trademark of Simplicity Pattern
    Co., Inc.
Soft Touch is a registered trademark of Fairfield Processing.
Styrofoam Brand Insulation is a registered trademark of
    Dow Chemical.
Sulky is a registered trademark of Sulky of America.
Ultrasuede is a registered trademark of Springs Industries.

The "Impressions" line of fabrics shown within the book
    design are courtesy of Benartex.

In appreciation:
Hobbs Bonded Fibers provided the batt for
    Jacobean Rhapsody No. 1
Fairfield Processing Corporation provided the batt for
    Jacobean Rhapsody No. 2
Sulky of America provided the quilting thread for
    Jacobean Rhapsodies No. 1 and *No. 2*

Published by C&T Publishing, Inc.
P.O. Box 1456
Lafayette, California 94549

Printed in China

10   9   8   7   6   5   4   3

Contents

Overture 5
WHY JACOBEAN? WHY APPLIQUÉ?
WHY RHAPSODIES?

The Designs 1-28 .... 6 - 32

Compositions 33
Jacobean Rhapsody No. 1 34
Jacobean Rhapsody No. 2 35
Jacobean Rhapsody No. 3 38
Jacobean Rhapsody No. 4 39
Jacobean Rhapsody No. 5 40
Jacobean Rhapsody No. 6 41
Jacobean Rhapsody No. 7 42
Jacobean Rhapsody No. 8 43
Jacobean Rhapsody No. 9 44
Jacobean Rhapsody No. 10 45

Improvisation 46

Instruments 48

Bar Staff 50
Fabric • Master Pattern Material •
Template Material • Batting • Thread

Tuning Up 52
Criteria • Making the Master Pattern •
Cutting the Background Fabric • Marking the
Background Fabric • Making Templates •
Marking and Cutting Design Pieces • Cutting and
Making Bias • Not Marking the Background
Fabric • Basting

Performance 55
Appliqué • Hand Method • Curves • Points •
Circles • Deep "V's" • Scallops • Tulips • Butting •
Machine Method • Heat Bonding Method

Finale 60
Assembling the Quilt • Mitering the Border •
Cutting the Backing • Quilting • Quilt Sleeve •
Binding • Mitering the Binding

Composer 63

Applause 63

Patterns 64
Design 1: Queen's Lace 66
Design 2: Primrose Tree 69
Design 3: Trumpet Tulips 73
Design 4: Mayfair Grapes 79
Design 5: Pixie Vine 81
Design 6: Canterbury Bells........82
Design 7: Lancaster Oak Leaf 86
Design 8: Oxford Oak 90
Design 9: Worcester Pomegranate.........91
Design 10: Derby Swirl 94
Design 11: Chelsea Wattle 96
Design 12: Tulip Berry 100
Design 13: Tulip Swirl 102
Design 14: Scarlet Cherry 103
Design 15: Cambridge Vines 106
Design 16: Wind Tree 110
Design 17: Heart Vine 116
Design 18: Painted Hearts........117
Design 19: Snow Heath 119
Design 20: Newcastle Vine 123
Design 21: Sweetbriar 127
Design 22: Windsor Sunflower.....128
Design 23: Passion Vine 131
Design 24: Lancaster Tulip 133
Design 25: Silky Oak 136
Design 26: Fairy Apron 138
Design 27 (Border): Queen's Garden 139
Design 28 (Border): Queen's Garden 147

Scores 156-159
Jacobean Rhapsody No. 3–10

Bibliography 160

Index................................... 160

Pat dedicates Jacobean Rhapsodies
in memory of

　　Douglas Vernon Campbell, Sr.

　　…we laughed, we loved, we lived!

　　My mentor, my champion, my best friend, my biggest fan, my true love.

　　He was the "wind beneath my wings." They flutter no more.

Mimi dedicates Jacobean Rhapsodies *to*

　　three fine needlewomen—

　　three finer friends—

　　Pam, Sadako, and Sharry.

Heroes of yore were knights in shining armor or lords on prancing horses. A hero of today is the Prince of Rhapsody, Randy Silvers, who came forth on his quilting machine and quilted *Jacobean Rhapsody No. 1* and *Jacobean Rhapsody No. 2* out of the goodness of his royal heart. His castle, Fran's Quilt Shop, Greensboro, NC, has no moat, but, instead, an open door with the Prince himself there to greet you.

"Appliqué is rhapsody, music to my eyes."

Why Jacobean?

Jacobean refers to the elegant, artful embroidery that originated within the reign of Queen Elizabeth I of England. The style continued to be a prominent artform for the following 100 years, through the Stuart successors from King James I to Queen Anne. Though the term "Jacobean" was not used until many years after the death of King James, the name derives from his formal title, "Jacobus Britanniae Rex." This is the king of the King James version of the Bible; this is the period of Shakespeare; it is also the time of the early migration of settlers from England to the American colonies.

When the settlers came to New England, they brought some of their treasures with them. Designs were adapted to the new culture and the times, and Jacobean embroidery became known in America as "crewel work." Exquisite needlework designs of rolling hillocks, sweeping branches, graceful leaves, swirling vines, and exotic flowers were embroidered on linen with soft, slackly twisted, two-ply worsted yarn of brilliant colors. Such items as bed coverlets, table covers, chair seats, cushions, swags, dresses, and petticoats became family heirlooms handed down from generation to generation.

For *Jacobean Rhapsodies*, Pat Campbell has adapted 28 of these marvelous designs for you to compose your rhapsody, using fabric rather than yarn. Just as Jacobean embroidery gave the needlewoman of old an opportunity to express her individuality, so Jacobean appliqué today gives you an opportunity to express your individuality. Let your imagination and creativity guide you when using these designs and for the compositions you create.

Why Appliqué?

Appliqué is the ancient and universal practice of applying one material to the surface of another for the purpose of embellishment. The practice goes back in time perhaps to Adam and Eve, who may have decorated their dull green leaves with colorful blossoms. Appliqué, a passion of Pat's, lends itself to maintaining the spirit of Jacobean embroidery, yet employs a different needleart medium.

Why Rhapsodies?

In musical terms rhapsody refers to a composition not bound by established rules, and is suggestive of improvisation. Jacobean appliqué, as a descendent of a classical form of embroidery, and rhapsody, as a classical form of music, make good partners. Music calms the body and mind but excites the spirit. Listen to music—your kind of music—as you work with fabric, color, and stitching to enhance your creativity and skill.

The word "rhapsody" is also used to describe "exaggerated enthusiasm" and "extravagance of ideas and expressions." This book includes 10 Jacobean Rhapsodies. The first two compositions show all 28 designs while the other eight are variations on a theme. With *Jacobean Rhapsodies* as your guide, you can look forward to experiencing rhapsody as you orchestrate your projects.

Improvise! Rhapsodize!

QUEEN'S LACE

DESIGN 1
Pattern on page 66.

"Many people tell me that what I do must take patience and be stressful. For me, quilting (especially appliqué) is the opposite—a relaxing form of therapy that draws out creativity and makes me feel fulfilled."

*Stitched by Jane McCabe,
Sheboygan Falls, WI.*

DESIGN 2

Pattern on page 69.

"I enjoy appliquéing and most of my projects

involve hand stitching. Thanks for the opportunity

to use such fun colors in a beautiful design."

Stitched by Deborah L. Cadwallender,
Crown Point, IN.

TRUMPET TULIPS

DESIGN 3
Pattern on page 73.

"Even though I'm a 'pastel' woman, I enjoyed working with a

riot of colors. Quilting is my link to tranquillity."

Stitched by Martha Caterino,
East Lansing, MI.

MAYFAIR GRAPES

DESIGN 4
Pattern on page 79.

"Fifteen years of quilting has been a very important part of who I am. It allows me to create, using color, shape, and fabric. The nicest people I know are those I've met through quilting."

Stitched by Judy Wagner, Bloomington, IN.

Design 5
PIXIE VINE

DESIGN 5
Pattern on page 81.

"I've been a needleart enthusiast for 16 years...appliqué speaks to my soul. The use of strong color and flowing design in Jacobean appliqué make it a true joy, soothing and exciting at the same time."

Stitched by Sheila Bird, Sheridan, AR.

CANTERBURY BELLS

DESIGN 6
Pattern on page 82.

"I love all kinds of

quiltmaking, especially

handwork. Working on this

block was a challenge

and a joy."

Stitched by Virginia
Anderson, Flushing, MI.

LANCASTER OAK LEAF

DESIGN 7
Pattern on page 86.

"It's true what they say:

quiltmaking is addictive.

I'm hooked on appliqué."

Stitched by Ann McCourt,
Lansing, MI.

OXFORD OAK

DESIGN 8
Pattern on page 90.

"I have been quilting since 1980. Dimensional and Baltimore Album appliqué have been my favorites. Now with Jacobean I enjoy another form of appliqué."

Stitched by Verona R. Johnson, Winter Haven, FL.

WORCESTER POMEGRANATE

DESIGN 9
Pattern on page 91.

"Jacobean appliqué is one of the most fascinating,

challenging, and intriguing of all the needlearts.

It's been great fun working on this project."

Stitched by Betty Foote,
Harrison, MI.

DERBY SWIRL

DESIGN 10
Pattern on page 94.

"What a privilege and a challenge to make this block.

The glorious colors and freedom of design are wonderful."

Stitched by Sara P. Hill,
Asheville, NC.

CHELSEA WATTLE

DESIGN 11
Pattern on page 96.

"Quilting is a major part of my well being. I receive a great deal of

satisfaction knowing I did all the work...it was a labor of love."

Stitched by C. Louise Fox,
State College, PA.

TULIP BERRY

DESIGN 12
Pattern on page 100.

"An introduction to quilting in 1983 changed my life. I have reaped the

rewards of meeting people from all walks of life, of friendships held together

with stitches, and of getting in touch with our foremothers and their creativity."

Stitched by Jane (Walters)
Oravetz, Montello, WI.

TULIP SWIRL

DESIGN 13
Pattern on page 102.

"It's no surprise that I'm attracted to Jacobean appliqué since I wrote a

thesis of a seventeenth-century Jacobean tapestry for my minor in art

history. Jacobean designs are wonderfully suited to appliqué."

Stitched by Kristen Schlactus,
Sherwood, OR.

SCARLET CHERRY

DESIGN 14
Pattern on page 103.

"Textiles have always been a large part of my life, but in the last 10 years appliqué and quilting have been the outlet for my creative urges. I love every aspect of the process from design to completion."

Stitched by Terri Willett, Fairfax, VA.

CAMBRIDGE VINES

DESIGN 15
Pattern on page 106.

"I love to appliqué and consider it great 'basket' therapy.

Jacobean appliqué can get very bright with color."

Stitched by Geraldine A. Vieaux,
Rhinelander, WI.

WIND TREE

DESIGN 16
Pattern on page 110.

"Although a beginning appliquér, I felt confident enough to stitch this block. Surprise,

it was fun! Jacobean designs with their gorgeous colors are wonderful inspiration."

Stitched by Vanessa A. Haese,
Rhinelander, WI.

HEART VINE

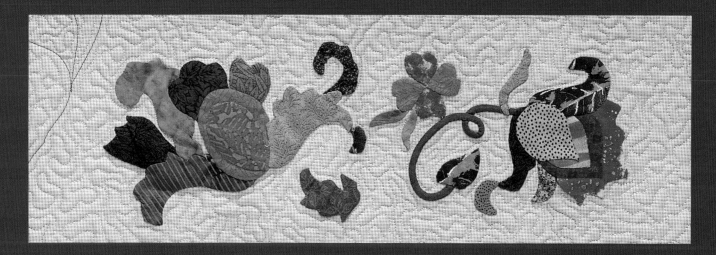

DESIGN 17
Pattern on page 116.

"Quiltmaking has been a part of my life for as long as I can remember. I feel fortunate to have had one of the best teachers, my mother. It was a pleasure and joy to stitch the Jacobean appliqué block."

Stitched by Florence Edwards, Woolrich, PA.

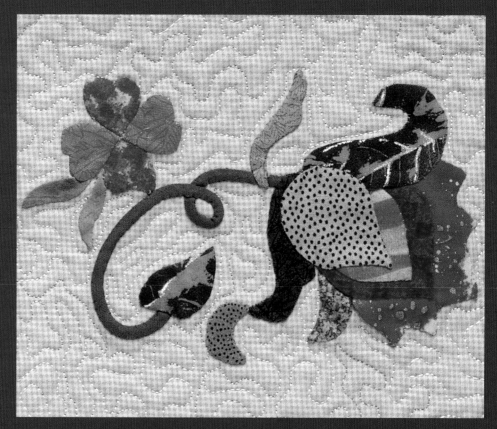

PAINTED HEARTS

DESIGN 18
Pattern on page 117.

"I especially enjoy hand

appliqué because I can take my

work with me. I'm not tied to a

machine in a room by myself.

I find the rich colors of Jacobean

appliqué especially exciting."

*Stitched by Debra Botelho
Zeida, Waquoit, MA.*

SNOW HEATH

DESIGN 19
Pattern on page 119.

"Quilting and appliqué

have become a way of life

for me. Jacobean appliqué

is a challenge that becomes

a lovely work of art."

Stitched by Judy Gammell,
Reading, PA.

NEWCASTLE VINE

DESIGN 20
Pattern on page 123.

"After discovering the world of quiltmaking, I composed a verse to express what it means to me: Quilting is cloth and stitches, made with loving wishes…creative expressions that calm the nerves, soothe the worries, provide comfort and pride..."

Stitched by Carole Sutton, Lowell, IN.

S W E E T B R I A R

DESIGN 21
Pattern on page 127.

"My first love is appliqué. Jacobean appliqué has fueled my imagination. I'll probably never be able to do all the projects I've dreamed up, but to complete a third of them would make me happy."

Stitched by Latricia Sargent, Cotopaxi, CO.

WINDSOR SUNFLOWER

DESIGN 22
Pattern on page 128.

"I began quiltmaking in 1990. I love all

aspects from handwork to machine. I fell in

love with Jacobean appliqué just looking at

the colors and contrasts and enjoying the

handwork while I'm traveling."

Stitched by Janice Cook,
Northville, MI.

PASSION VINE

DESIGN 23
Pattern on page 131.

"The vibrant contrast in colors makes Jacobean appliqué

exciting to create. I had such fun making this piece I can't

wait to see the whole quilt."

Stitched by Pam McCabe,
East Lansing, MI.

LANCASTER TULIP

DESIGN 24
Pattern on page 133.

"Quilts, like children, have minds of their own, but if we love them, listen to

them, and work with them, we can expect satisfying, if surprising, results."

Stitched by Michelle McLean,
Washington, MI.

SILKY OAK

DESIGN 25
Pattern on page 136.

"Quilting is one medium that is ever changing and leaves room for all types of creativity from traditional to modern art. Participating in this book is one of the highlights in my quilting career."

Stitched by Lynn M. Van Nest, Chelsea, MI.

DESIGN 26
Pattern on page 138.

"…I've found my true obsession in appliqué."

Stitched by Kristen Schlactus,
Sherwood, OR.

QUEEN'S GARDEN

DESIGN 27
Pattern on page 139.

"The designs and vibrant colors sing out the glories of Jacobean appliqué. Rhapsody! That's what it was to play a part in introducing this new design to the quilting world."

Stitched by Mary E. Wheatley,
Mashpee, MA.

DESIGN 28
Pattern on page 147.

"A new appliqué addict, I feel very honored to have had the pleasure of working on the border with its jewel-tone palette."

Stitched by Barbara A. Hamrin,
Falmouth, MA.

Design 27 (upper)

Design 27 (lower)

Design 28 top (left)

Design 28 top (right)

Like musical rhapsodies, each Jacobean Rhapsody sets a mood. The first two Jacobean Rhapsodies present a total of 28 designs. Every block in *Jacobean Rhapsody No. 1*— four squares and nine rectangles — has a twin in *Jacobean Rhapsody No. 2* in terms of size, yet every one of the designs is different. This allows you to choose a design from one Rhapsody and interchange it in the "twin" block space of another. One difference is that *Jacobean Rhapsody No. 2* has an appliquéd border on two sides, which means two border designs as well as 26 block designs.

You may reduce or enlarge the designs to fit, since size and proportion of the design relate to your project size. You can create a new block by rearranging the components of the design, by using part of a design or by combining parts of several designs. You can mix your choice of fabric type or color palette. Then you can decide if you want to hand appliqué, machine appliqué, or use an iron-on method.

If you are a novice, we encourage you to try Design 13 (page 102) or Design 17 (page 116). The patterns for these two designs suggest an order of stitching to get you started. Keep in mind that you can always change a detail if you think it's too hard to stitch; for example, make a leaf point more rounded. Let the illustrations and photographs guide you.

You can find a variety of ideas for projects from antique textiles embellished with Jacobean embroidery. You'll often discover examples in museums of embellished bed spreads, valances, cushions, chair seats, dresses, petticoats, and purses. Modern examples are wall quilts, table runners, placemats, pillows, vests, jackets, and even bridal trims.

A musical score contains the parts for performing a musical composition. Jacobean Rhapsody "scores" are provided so that you can "play the notes" as presented or interpret them in a new composition. The horizontal measurement is given first, then the vertical measurement.

JACOBEAN RHAPSODY NO.1

Designed by Pat Campbell, 64"x 64"; the score shown on page 36.

Jacobean Rhapsody No.1 *with its shades of aubergine and burgundy, textured "damask" background and sashing evokes a feeling of aristocracy. Its classic style, its traditional grace and beauty, its melody of colorful notes—smooth as satin, luxurious as velvet, and magnificent as silk—exude elegance.*

JACOBEAN RHAPSODY NO. 2

Designed by Pat Campbell, 68" x 68"; the score shown on page 37.

Jacobean Rhapsody No. 2 *effects a feeling of romance. In a garden of exotic blooming flowers, delicate vines creeping up a castle wall, and butterflies floating above the blossoms, all that's missing is a loving couple to walk its paths.*

The Score for J A C O B E A N   R H A P S O D Y   N O .   1

QUILT	64" x 64"
SASHING	2" wide, finished
BORDER	2" wide, finished
BINDING	¼" wide, finished

Design	Design Size	Cut Size*	Finished Size
1	22 ½" x 9 ¾"	27" x 11"	26" x 10"
2	8 ¼" x 25 ½"	11" x 29"	10" x 28"
3	18" x 17 ½"	21" x 21"	20" x 20"
4	15 ¼" x 5 ½"	19" x 7"	18" x 6"
5	14" x 5 ½"	17" x 7"	16" x 6"
6	12 ¼" x 16 ¾"	15" x 21"	14" x 20"
7	11" x 16 ¾"	15" x 21"	14" x 20"
8	13 ½" x 3 ¾"	15" x 5"	14" x 4"
9	8 ¼" x 24 ¼"	11" x 27"	10" x 26"
10	5 ¾" x 18"	7" x 21"	6" x 20"
11	12 ¾" x 13"	15" x 15"	14" x 14"
12	11" x 11 ¼"	13" x 13"	12" x 12"
13	7 ¼" x 7 ¼"	9" x 9"	8" x 8"

*After the block is appliquéd, add a ¼" seam allowance to all four sides of
the Finished Size, then trim the extra fabric from the edges.*

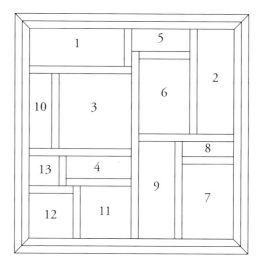

*Yardage: 3 yds of dark fabric for
background, border, and binding,
and 2 yds of light fabric for sashing*

Jacobean Rhapsodies

The Score for J A C O B E A N   R H A P S O D Y   N O .   2

QUILT	68" x 68"
SASHING	2" wide, finished
BORDER	two 2" wide, finished and two 10" wide, finished
BINDING	¼" wide, finished

Design	Design Size	Cut Size*	Finished Size
14	22 ½" x 9"	27" x 11"	26" x 10"
15	8" x 26"	11" x 29"	10" x 28"
16	17 ½" x 17"	21" x 21"	20" x 20"
17	14" x 4 ⅝"	19" x 7"	18" x 6"
18	14" x 6"	17" x 7"	16" x 6"
19	12 ½" x 18"	15" x 21"	14" x 20"
20	13" x 18 ½"	15" x 21"	14" x 20"
21	12" x 3 ½"	15" x 5"	14" x 4"
22	7 ½" x 22 ½"	11" x 27"	10" x 26"
23	5" x 18"	7" x 21"	6" x 20"
24	13" x 13"	15" x 15"	14" x 14"
25	10 ¼" x 11"	13" x 13"	12" x 12"
26	7" x 6 ½"	9" x 9"	8" x 8"
27 (Side Border)	8 ½" x 58 ½"	11" x 71"	10" x 68"
28 (Top Border)	8 ½" x 64"	11" x 71"	10" x 68"

*After the block is appliquéd, add a ¼" seam allowance to all four sides of
the Finished Size, then trim the extra fabric from the edges.

*Trim the width of the border after appliquéing and trim the ends after mitering.

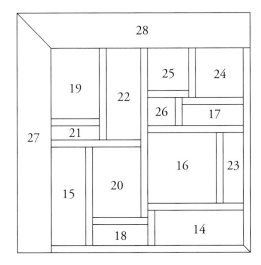

*Yardage: 5 yds of light fabric for
background, sashing, and borders*

JACOBEAN RHAPSODY NO. 3

Hand appliquéd by Lynn Van Nest, and hand quilted by Laura Rapa, 23" x 32"; the score shown on page 156.

This composition, created in the spirit of a musical rhapsody's free form, combines elements from several designs. An effective detail is the outline quilting ⅛ " outside the design in the color of that part of the design. "Participating in this book," says Lynn, "is one of the highlights of my quilting career."

JACOBEAN RHAPOSDY NO. 4

Designed and hand appliquéd by Pat Campbell, hand quilted by Bea Ribblett, 23" x 23";
the score shown on page 156.

This enchanting Rhapsody bears the imprint of a Campbell design in grace of line and drama of color.
The use of various shades of red and purple are dramatically set off by the eggshell background.
Invigorate the wreath, as Pat did, by choosing for the border one of the colors used in your block and for
the binding a color that contrasts. Quilted or unquilted, this design would make a lovely framed textile.
Imagine it in red and green on your front door for the holidays.

JACOBEAN RHAPSODY NO. 5

Hand appliquéd and hand quilted by Jane McCabe, 49" x 49"; the score shown on page 157.

Jane's orchestration and performance of this composition is flawless. Note her skill in the magnificently executed very narrow bias stems and vines. Sweet serenity results from the combination of tan-on-eggshell background, low-key multicolors in the appliqué, patterned leaf sashing, patterned plum binding, cross-hatch and outline quilting in beige thread and green thread within the designs and sashing. "Quilting is a relaxing form of therapy," says Jane, "that draws out creativity and makes me feel fulfilled."

JACOBEAN RHAPSODY NO. 6

Hand appliquéd, hand and machine quilted by Michelle McLean, 20" x 34"; the score shown on page 157.

In the spirit of rhapsodic freedom, Michelle has created a contemporary composition of an antique form. Hand appliqué, machine piecing, hand and machine quilting with metallic thread link the old and the new. The three touches of metallic fabric highlight the composition. "This quilt was intended to be a Christmas quilt — red, green, and gold —but it kept insisting on purple, then refused most of the reds and called for a touch of copper," says Michelle.

JACOBEAN RHAPSODY NO. 7

Hand appliquéd, hand embroidered, and hand quilted by Betty Foote, 32" x 32";
the score shown on page 158.

The middle quartet, making a medallion, the embroidered vine instead of bias, and the use of design
fabrics in the binding make for a visual musical melody in Betty's composition. "Jacobean appliqué is
one of the most fascinating, challenging, and intriguing of all the needlearts," says Betty.

Jacobean Rhapsodies

JACOBEAN RHAPSODY NO. 8

Hand appliquéd and hand quilted by Sharon Chambers, 50" x 39 ½"; the score shown on page 158.

Sharon's composition in a three-part Rhapsody triggers warm emotions. Its brown on eggshell background, blue-green and purple leaf patterned border, hand-dyed hot pink sashing, and a meandering quilting design portray a whimsical rhapsody. Sharon comments, "I love Jacobean appliqué! The pieces are so easy to appliqué and the look is so nice."

JACOBEAN RHAPSODY NO. 9

Hand appliquéd and hand quilted by Geraldine A. Vieaux, 42" x 42"; the score shown on page 159.

Geri created a striking composition that pulsates with rhythm: note the block set on-point, the design in opposite corners, the variety of quilting patterns, and the variegated fabric for the binding. "I love to appliqué…I consider it great 'basket' therapy."

JACOBEAN RHAPSODY NO. 10

Hand appliquéd by Betty Young, assembled by Beth C. Anderson, hand quilted by
Sharon Woodard, 30" x 30"; the score shown on page 159.

Jacobean Rhapsody No. 10 *bombards the senses and sends drums beats through the breast.*
Change the center design fabric to see what a difference fabric can make.

Improvisation

Jumper by Rhonda Bellamy Hodge; skirt border, Design 27; top, Design 5; machine appliquéd and machine embroidered, unquilted; Jacket by Beth Anderson; flower from Design 7; machine appliquéd and quilted

The jumper is one of Rhonda's original "Comfortable Jumper" patterns from Hodge-Podge Gifts & Accessories.

Beth made the jacket from Pat's collection of "Impressions" fabric by Benartex as a surprise for her. The embellishment sends it into orbit — wild, fun, attention-getting, pizzazz for any outfit. "Combining the art of Jacobean appliqué with wearables is a new venture for me," said Beth.

Vest by Sheila Bird; Design 5 and 16, hand appliquéd, un-quilted; "The use of strong color and flowing design in Jacobean appliqué make it a true joy, soothing and exciting at the same time."

Sheila made this beautiful vest for her 12-year old daughter, who helped choose the fabrics. She used a basic vest pattern (Simplicity® pattern 9630), embellishing it with "notes" from several Jacobean Rhapsody designs.

Jacket, Jacobean Rhapsody in Silk,

by Alexandra Capadalis Dupré;

elements of Design 5 repositioned, silk ribbon embroidered, un-quilted; "Jacobean appliqué designs inspired me to take the silk ribbon technique beyond the traditional boundaries of small flora and fauna."

Alex used simple stitches such as a split stitch, feather stitch, and Japanese ribbon stitch for her silk ribbon embroidery. Over 100 yards of ribbon, donated by Sharee Dawn Roberts, Web of Thread, Paducah, KY, were required. It took 60 hours to embroider this exquisite white linen jacket.

Bell Pull by Kathleen Anderson; scattered grapes and leaves from Design 15, hand appliquéd and hand quilted. Tote by Mitzi Golub and Jamie McArthur-Engle; Design 25, hand appliquéd by Mitzi (unquilted) and made into a tote by Jamie. Placemats and Hosiery Case, Design 21; Photo Album Cover, Design 13; and Gift Wine Sack, Design 15 are examples of items for heat bonding that were made by anonymous volunteers.

A bell pull can be an object of beauty, useless today except to show off an appliquér's expertise; use any of the repeat designs. Try Design 27 or 28 for a table runner or a mantle quilt. You'll be surprised how this one piece of needlework will change the look of your table or your room. Machine appliqué and machine quilting will minimize the time invested and the result will be very attractive. These patterns can also be used for a piano bench cushion, window valances, curtain borders, and tie backs. Designs 3, 11, 12, 16, 24, 25 lend themselves to pillow tops, framed textiles, even fireplace screens.

Instruments

Most quiltmakers own many tools, usually kept in a box, a basket, or a drawer. These always include the essentials, such as needles and pins. For many they include a gaggle of gadgets. Check the following to see what tools we like to have on hand:

NEEDLES

The shorter the needle the better, because a short needle is stronger than a long one. (Why push more steel than is needed again and again through a piece of fabric?) If you learn to appliqué, sew, and quilt with the same size needle, then you save re-learning time, which means you can undertake more projects. Size 12 or 10 Betweens is recommended; we suggest the Clover® brand. However, use any size needle that feels right to you. Consider having a number of needles in use at the same time whether appliquéing or quilting.

♪ *Shorter is better.*

PINS AND PIN CUSHION

A variety of pins is helpful. Brightly colored glass-headed pins, like sashiko and quilting, help you to find them should they become "lost." If you like to use short pins (thinking they will be less in your way as you stitch), use the thinnest ones you can find. The new sequin pins, sometimes labeled "appliqué pins," found in many quilt shops are great. Avoid the old sequin pins which are thick and blunt; these pins were intended for attaching sequins to Styrofoam® balls.

♪ *What's a magnet?*
A detective that finds "lost" pins.

SCISSORS

Two pairs are a must. You need small sharp scissors, such as the Gingher® 4" Embroidery, for cutting the fabric of your design pieces, and template cutting scissors, like the Fiskars® 5" Sharp Point, to spare your sharp ones.

THIMBLE

If you do not wear a thimble, try one now. Students claim they learned to use one in a week's time and now cannot stitch without one. All fingers deserve protection but especially the "pushing" finger. It's no exaggeration to say the middle finger goes through the same motion over 500 times every hour you stitch. In addition, because of the smallness of the needle, the risk is high that the eye end will puncture again and again an unprotected finger. Ouch!

♪ *Stay unstuck with a thimble.*

LAMP

You want your appliqué stitches small and hidden; you want your quilting stitches even. If you can't see, you can't produce work to be proud of. Therefore, be sure you're sitting where the light hits directly on your work. A 72-watt halogen bulb is cooler than a regular bulb and lets you run the air-conditioning more economically. Try the Ott-Light® for convenient natural light.

GLASSES

If you need glasses, forget vanity and wear them. You can always tuck them under your work if there's a knock at the door.

♪ *Seeing is relieving.*

SANDPAPER BOARD

Once you have used a sandpaper board you will never again draw around a template on fabric without one. No wiggling and no distortion results because the sandpaper keeps the fabric from moving. You can make an inexpensive and portable "board" by gluing a piece of fine sandpaper to the inside of a file folder or onto a clipboard.

♪ *Sandpaper board's an extra hand.*

PENCILS

You will need a mechanical and a chalk or white charcoal pencil, the first to mark on light fabrics and the latter to mark on dark fabrics. A mechanical pencil always has a sharp point. If you prefer colored pencils, try Berol Prismacolor®. A drawback is that they have soft lead and must be sharpened often. Be cautious about using a yellow pencil; some have a wax base that becomes permanent when hit by heat.

PENS

A permanent pen or a washable one can be used to draw the template, depending on whether you like a dark edge or a clean edge. Try a Sanford Sharpie® with an ultrafine point. Another choice, if you like a clear template, is a mechanical pencil with a #2 lead that can be erased.

ERASER

If you follow the instructions carefully, rare should be the occasion for an eraser. However, it would be wise, just in case, to try different erasers on a scrap of your background fabric before you mark the pattern. Should you find you do need to erase, even after painstaking efforts to avoid making marks that show, you will know which one works best. Different types of fabric affect the ease or difficulty of erasing. Try a Pentel Clic™ eraser. A student suggested rubbing out unwanted lines with a clean rubber finger; just be sure to experiment with a scrap before trying it on your project. Some say hair spray will remove pencil marks: spray lightly, let dry, and rub with an eraser. Again, try it on a scrap before using it on your quilt.

LIGHTBOX

Tracing a pattern on a dark background is impossible without light showing through the fabric. Tracing on a light background is much easier with back lighting. Yes, a purchased light-box is expensive, but you can improvise by using a glass-top table with a lamp set under it or a table with leaves pulled apart with a plastic or glass desk protector laid across the surface and a lamp underneath. Of course, there is always the old-fashioned way: tape the fabric to a window glass.

STYROFOAM PANELS

Depending on the size of your wall, purchase one or more 4' x 8' Styrofoam panels. When covered with flannel and attached to a wall, these panels are invaluable for "reading" your composition for color, texture, balance, harmony, contrast. The pieces will speak to you, "I'm beautiful" or "I'm a nice color, but not in this location." If space is not available, make a 4' x 4' portable panel and store it under the bed or in the garage when it's not in use.

♪ *Inexpensive! Invaluable!*

CIRCLE TEMPLATE

The variety of circle sizes in a commercial template purchased at an office supply store lets you choose a size close to the circles shown in the printed designs. Drawing inside a circle template onto your template plastic is easier than tracing the circle from the printed pattern and will probably be more round. Coins make excellent templates for circles.

EMERY BOARD

Since you want your circle templates to be as near perfectly round as possible, you can file off any little jags with an emery board.

BIAS MAKING GADGET

Bias strips of fabric are used for vines and very curvy stems. A bias press bar, a Celtic Bias Bar®, Fasturn®, or your sewing machine adapter can be used. Follow the manufacturer's instructions. Try them all to see which one you like best.

T-SQUARE

A constant concern for quiltmakers is keeping their work square. A T-square is a good investment to guarantee that your work is squared up, reducing the possibility of dipping and sagging. These range from inexpensive to very expensive. Shop building supply and office supply stores for the best buys.

RULER, SEWING MACHINE, IRON, IRONING BOARD, ROTARY CUTTER AND PAD

These important items are common in quiltmakers' homes. Little needs to be said about them. They are essential.

COMFORTABLE CHAIR

Create a stitching "nest" for many hours of pleasure stitching. Seat yourself in a chair that fits. Then put your feet up. This makes you lean back, not forward—placing you in a relaxed position. When you are comfortable with your back well supported and your derriere well padded, you can stitch for many many happy hours.

Now that you've gathered all the necessary tools in one place, you're ready to look at your fabric collection.

FABRIC

Type

One hundred percent cotton for the background fabric and the backing is recommended. You can use all cotton, blended cotton, polyester, linen, silk, rayon, wool, velvet, felt, Ultrasuede®, or a combination of these for the design pieces. Each has its strengths and weaknesses, which affect the ease or difficulty in handling, the choice of appliqué method, and the final appearance. Overall, 100% cotton is the BEST choice. Blended cotton and man-made fabrics are hard to needle turn because they don't like to stay folded under. Silk is beautiful with a magic tactile quality, but wrinkles when pressed and tends to flatten. Linen, velvet, and wool are heavy and fray. Felt and Ultrasuede work well with machine appliqué. Experiment with mixing textiles and/or mixing appliqué techniques. Try any that interest you; experiment with combining. Practice both machine and hand stitching on those you like. Discover which fabrics are easier to work with and which ones you find more attractive.

Color

Some people have an ear for music; some people have an eye for color. Some may have no training, yet are unable to explain their talent. Those who are not so gifted can learn—through study, trial and error, and following the work of people like Pat who have inborn color sense.

♪ *Choose the background fabric first.*

If you choose the background fabric first, it will be easier to combine the pieces in terms of color, print, and texture. Neutral backgrounds — beige, white, light yellow, black, navy — give you more freedom in combining the fabrics for your design pieces, but consider experimenting with other shades.

♪ *Color is personal.*

Choose colors that you like. Color is personal. What is flashy to one person is dull to another. If you adore pastels, use them, but know your work will lack the pizzazz you get when you combine brilliants and subtles. Solids look flat compared to a mixture of small and large prints. A few solids with mostly printed fabrics is fine, but a few printed fabrics with mostly solids will trap the eye in the prints. As with music, harmony is needed for Jacobean Rhapsodies. But, harmony does not mean matching. Matching is at best ho-hum and at worst, boring.

♪ *Coordinate is "out", contrast is "in".*

Contrast breathes life into the body of the composition: contrast in the size of the print, contrast in intensity, in value, in temperature, and in texture. Include large prints, such as tropicals, which add action; hand-dyes, which add highlights; and florals, paisleys, and chintzes, which add movement. Two colors of the same intensity vibrate, yet if one is strong and one is weak, each enhances the other. Brilliants are wonderful, but, if not in contrast to subtles, are overwhelming. Warm colors, like the reds and oranges, are in-your-face colors. Cool colors, like blues and greens, are laid back and can put you to sleep. A warm accent adds sparkle amid cool colors. The eye rather than the fingers stroke the surface of the fabric and respond with pleasure. Contrast suggests spontaneity, the spontaneity of the musical rhapsodic form.

♪ *Try fabrics in a chorus, never solo.*

Play with your fabrics, making different combinations. Pat likes to fold a piece she wants to use into a small roll, put others with it, and hold the "bundle" at arm's length. She then tries different combinations until she gets what she likes. She also wraps a little bit of the fabric around her finger like a rosebud and folds another piece around that. For her it's either an "aha" and goes into the project or it's a "nope" and she tries another.

After you have chosen your fabrics and cut the design pieces, pin them to the foamboard, then step back and squint. If you sit on top of an orchestra, you may hear only one instrument, but backing up lets you get a balanced effect. So with your composition, back up and view it from six feet away. An easy way to check on balance is to use the Rule of the Triangle. It's not a rule really, but a guide. Briefly, if a specific color falls at the three points of a triangle (right triangle, equilateral triangle, or isosceles triangle), in any position, there is balance. There can be any number of triangles.

♪ *The Rule of the Triangle is a guide.*

The Maestro of your Rhapsody is your eye. You'll know you've achieved a successful performance when your composition radiates life. Don't hesitate to remove a piece from your composition, even after it's stitched. If you don't like it, it will always remain a sour note.

The Hungarian rhapsodies by Litsz were inspired by the excitement he experienced hearing the melodic songs and feeling the dance rhythms of the Bohemians. You'll be inspired by the ten Jacobean Rhapsodies as you experience the exotic color combinations and the flowing movement of the designs. Study the photographs. Observe the color combinations. Check the contrasts. Notice the accents.

For a more thorough discussion of color and fabric see our book, *Jacobean Applique: Romantica*, pages 14-23.

Most quiltmakers have a treasure trove of fabric—in a closet, under a bed, in the trunk of a car. Now is the time to gather those pieces you think you want to use. If your stash is limited, exchange swatches with friends, trade with those in your bee and guild. Buy fat eighths or fat quarters, rather than yardage, because you want a small quantity and a wide variety. If you are timid about color combinations, use the photographs of the Rhapsodies as models. Then practice. Like a musician, practice improves your performance. The more Jacobean appliqué you do, the more confident you will become when combining colors.

MASTER PATTERN MATERIAL

For your master pattern use inexpensive lightweight nonwoven non-fusible interfacing. It usually comes in a package of three yards 15" wide. You can also buy it by the yard in a 45" width.

TEMPLATE MATERIAL

See-through template plastic available at quilt shops in 13" x 20" sheets lets you not only see to trace the templates from the printed pattern but also lets you see where to place them on the design fabric for the best results. You can also use tracing paper, freezer paper, butcher paper, or lightweight bond.

BATTING

Quiltmakers can be confused by the wide assortment of batts available on the market today. There are polyester, cotton, wool, and silk batts, and you can choose a variety within each category in terms of loft and finished surface. Learn all you can about the different options. Talk with friends about their experiences. Often at quilt shows there are samples to try. Consider whether you are machine quilting or hand quilting, how much quilting you want to do, what type of care will be required, how the item will be used, whether light or dark fabric shades are used in the top, and the cost of the product. Pat's favorites are Hobbs' Poly-Down® and Fairfield's Soft Touch®.

THREAD

Machine embroidery thread is best for hand appliqué because it's thin, hides well, and comes in a wide array of shades. Match the design piece, not the background. Avoid polyester thread because it can cut through the fabric. Silk is fine, and as with machine embroidery thread may be used on any fabric, but it is expensive and slides off the needle (which is very frustrating). For machine quilting try Mettler thread. Use quilting thread the same color as the background, because you don't want the quilting pattern to compete with the design.

♪ *Fine thread hides stitches.*

Before you begin your project, you have the opportunity to decide on a number of options: 1) choosing from 28 designs, 2) appliquéing by hand, machine, or iron-on, 3) marking or not marking background fabric, 4) using bias or embroidery for stems and vines, 5) squaring or mitering corners for borders, 6) quilting by hand or machine, and 7) selecting a binding method.

Any design can be used for any project. The design may be enlarged or reduced to fit the space you require. A section of a design may be used; or a part or the whole can be repeated, for example, for a border. An element can be turned in a different direction. The swirls can be altered. Use the designs however they please you. For purposes of illustrating the Jacobean appliqué basics, we'll use parts of different designs.

CRITERIA TO DETERMINE HAND APPLIQUÉ, MACHINE APPLIQUÉ, OR HEAT BONDING

1. Planned life of the item (single event vs. life-time)
2. Skill of machine appliquéing (novice vs. advanced)
3. Time crunch (next week vs. next year)
4. For whom the item is made (gift vs. self)
5. Use of item (heirloom wall quilt vs. T-shirt embellishment)
6. Attitude of maker (purist vs. utilitarian)

MAKING THE MASTER PATTERN

Trace the printed design pattern on a piece of interfacing that has been cut the same size as the background fabric (see Master Pattern Material, page 51). Mark the center of the design (⊕) to help center it on the background. Align the tic marks (−) and the vertical and horizontal broken lines.

CUTTING THE BACKGROUND FABRIC

Trim the selvage. If you're making a block from *Rhapsody No.1* or *Rhapsody No. 2*, cut the background fabric for each block according to the scores on pages 36 and 37. Note that there are cut and finished measurements for each. Example: the block for Design 1 is cut 27" x 11". After you appliqué this block, trim the block to 26 ½" x 10 ½" for a ¼" seam allowance. The

finished block size is 26" x 10". If you're making one of the variations, *Rhapsody No.3* through *Rhapsody No. 10*, see the score for that quilt (pages 156-159). If you are using a border or sashing of the same fabric as your block, consider cutting them now.

MARKING THE BACKGROUND FABRIC

You can choose to mark or not to mark the pattern on the background. If you choose marking, do it now. If not, look for the instructions on page 54 when you are ready to appliqué.

1. Find the center of the background fabric block by folding it in half first one way and then the other. Pinch the intersection, but don't mark.
2. Line up the center (⊕) of the master pattern and the center of the block with the background fabric on top, right side up. Square the two.
3. Mark lightly with pencil on the background fabric about ⅛" INSIDE the master pattern lines. This will give you a little "fudging" space. A lightbox makes the tracing easy but other means are suggested in Instruments (page 49).
4. A centered single line works well for a branch, tree trunk, stem, vine. Example: Design 2, Part 12 (tree trunk); Design 6 (bias stem); Design 12, Part 23 (branch); and Design 23 (bias vine).
5. Use an "x" for small pieces. Example: Design 5, Parts 1, 2, 3, and 5.

Appliqué is fun because it doesn't require the exact positioning that piecing does.

MAKING TEMPLATES

No template patterns appear in the book, except for the two tulips found on page 77 and page 127. You make your own templates by tracing the individual parts of the printed pattern onto see-through material (see Template Material on page 51.)

Number each piece with a permanent black fine-line pen (Example: "17-20" refers to Design 17, Part 20.) This way you will always know which side of the template is right side up and can easily separate them should parts of different designs get mixed. On some pattern parts you'll see an "R" added to a number assigned to another part. This tells you to turn it over to draw around it.

If the design piece for which you're making the template goes UNDER another piece and does not show in the printed pattern, be sure to draw it as if it were a complete part.

Carefully cut the templates, and place them in their proper position on the master pattern.

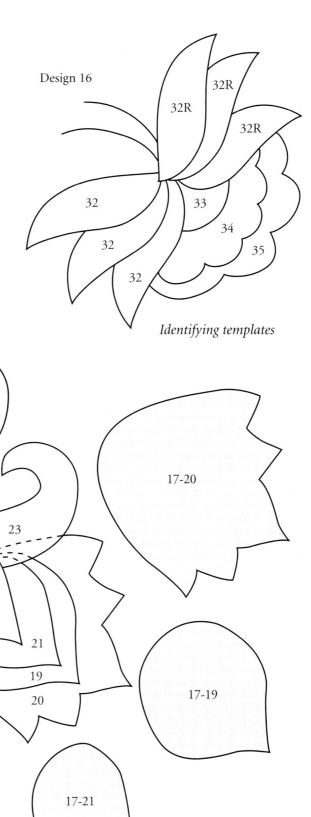

Design 16

Identifying templates

Design 17

Drawing complete templates

MARKING AND CUTTING DESIGN PIECES

Choose which fabrics will go where. With the sandpaper board (see Instruments, page 48) on the bottom, next the design fabric right side up, and the template on top, draw on the fabric around the template. Don't worry about grain. The more bias or near bias the better, especially for hand appliqué, because it makes needle-turning easier with less raveling. Mark the outline clearly because you can't needle-turn smoothly if you can't see the line. The line will not show as it rolls under when you stitch. Angle your pencil so the tip is as close to the template as possible, making your design piece more accurate and eliminating the annoyance of rippling the fabric as you trace.

If you're planning to hand appliqué, cut the pieces with an ⅛", yes, an ⅛" seam allowance for turn under. If planning to machine appliqué or heat bond, cut the pieces on the line. Position them on the master pattern and pin in place. This makes your project portable. Store the used templates in a small plastic bag, identified by the design number.

CUTTING AND MAKING BIAS

For stems and vines, cut bias strips with your rotary cutter, never less than 1". If less than 1" in width, the strips may wiggle while sewing and result in an uneven bias. Fold a perfect square on the true diagonal. Pin "here and there." Use a ruler that has a 45° line. Trim off ½" along the fold. The amount of bias needed will depend on the length and number of stems and/or vines that appear in the block. Be generous in the amount of bias you make. You want to be able to cut away joining seams because you don't want them to show on your appliqué. An 8" square will make about 50" of bias cut 1" in width; a 10" square, about 85". Leftovers can be used later. Store them wrapped around a paper towel cardboard core.

♪ *Save bias leftovers.*

You have a choice of how to make the strips: use a bias press bar, a Celtic Bias Bar, Fasturn, or your sewing machine adapter. Of course, there are old-fashioned gadgetless ways. One that has been around for generations is to fold the strip in thirds with one raw edge inside and one underneath. Another traditional way is to fold the raw edges together right side out. Then machine sew a seam a little less than ¼" from the raw edges. You can make the bias more narrow by sewing closer to the fold and trimming away the excess. Cover the raw edges with the fold, then pin, and appliqué in place.

As an alternative, the stems, vines, and tendrils can be embroidered as in *Rhapsody No. 3* and *Rhapsody No. 7*. You choose the stitch and the shade of embroidery floss.

NOT MARKING THE BACKGROUND FABRIC

This method can be used for hand, machine, or heat bonding appliqué.
1. Lay the master pattern, with the pieces pinned in place, over the right side of the background fabric.
2. Match the center of the pattern and the background fabric, square up, and baste the two together only across the top.

♪ *No marking. No erasing.*

3. Remove a "bottom-layer" design piece from the master pattern, and pin it in its appropriate position under the master pattern on the background fabric.
4. Lift the master pattern, flipping it over the top. Then appliqué the design piece in place.
5. Continue with another piece or a small cluster of pieces.

♪ *Put pins on WRONG side.*

BASTING

Generally, you don't have to baste the design pieces to the background fabric. A pin or two should hold a piece in place until you stitch the piece by hand or machine. A touch of the iron will anchor a piece for heat bonding. You may, however, want to thread-baste tree trunks because they may shift (Example: Design 9, Part 11, page 91). Small pieces can shift too, but ususally this is not serious. You can always add another leaf or flower or re-cut the piece, making it larger.

APPLIQUÉ

Appliqué means layering: a single piece or a number of pieces on top of another piece. Don't worry about how many layers. Layering will give your design depth, and generally you're not going to quilt within the parts of the design.

There are always "over" and "under" pieces. Some people like to do all the "unders" in a design first so they don't forget. Start with the very bottom piece

Design 17

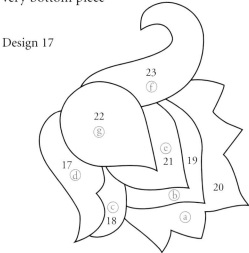

Stitching order: the numbers refer to the design parts, letters suggest order of stitching.

For those of you who are timid when deciding which piece to stitch first, look at the patterns for Design 13 and Design 17, where suggested stitching orders are given.

HAND METHOD

Pat is internationally known for her hand appliqué. Therefore, the discussion of this method will be more detailed than the machine or heat bonding appliqué method.

Starting

1. Cut a piece of machine embroidery thread only 15"-18" long. A short thread will be less likely to tangle or fray than a longer one. Remember to MATCH the design piece. If you can't match it, use a shade darker thread, not lighter.

♪ *Match thread to design piece, not background.*

2. Thread a #10 or #12 Betweens needle. If you have trouble threading your needle, try needling

your thread end or try wetting the needle eye, rather than the thread, with saliva. Knot the end.

3. Start anywhere in the design, except at a point. It is easiest to begin stitching on a straight-away or gentle curve. You don't need to stitch the part of the piece that goes under another piece.

♪ *Starting at a point is a no-no.*

Stitching

1. Place a pin on the WRONG side to hold the piece in place.
2. With the tip of the needle, sweep under approximately 1" of the seam allowance.
3. Hold the position with your thumbnail pressed tightly against the edge of the fold.

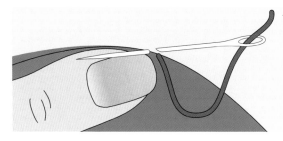

Position for stitching

4. Bring the needle up in that fold, hiding the knot.
5. Take a stitch straight out from that point into the background fabric. For the prettiest work with hidden stitches and without dimpling, always make your stitches into the background fabric PERPENDICULAR to the edge of the design piece.

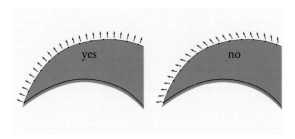

Perpendicular stitches

The arrows in the illustration show the angles of the stitches, not the distance from the fold. A stitch taken too far from the fold into the background fabric or a stitch taken too deep into the design piece will show. If the stitches slant they will not only show, but dimple the fabric as well.

6. Stitching counterclockwise (unless you are left handed), pick up two or three threads of the background fabric and come up in the edge of the fold about ⅛" away.

7. Continue, turning a small section of the seam allowance under, always with your needle, never with your fingers. Practice will teach you how much to turn under. Too long a needle sweep lets a bit sneak out; too short a sweep makes peaks. Usually, ¾"-1" width is just about right.

When a dark piece shows through a light piece, sandwich between them a buffer of organdy or muslin which has been cut with no seam allowance.

Stopping

1. When your thread becomes too short to continue, put the needle through to the back of the background fabric away from the design edge.

2. Pick up a tiny bit of the fabric without coming through to the front. Pull up gently without puckering. Repeat.

3. Bury the thread about ½" from the second stitch. Snip off the tail.

CONVEX (OUTSIDE) CURVES

These make for the easiest stitching of all, except on a straight-away. You don't need to clip. The seam allowance is only ⅛" so it turns under easily. Stitching order: 12, 10, 11, and 7.

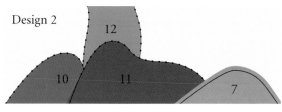

Convex curves

CONCAVE (INSIDE) CURVES

These are a little harder and occasionally you will have to clip, but do it ONLY when you feel a drag on the needle or the seam allowance won't stay under.

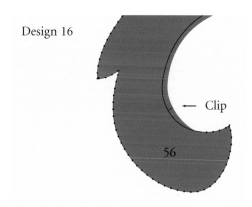

Concave curve

When there are two curves—a convex one and a concave one that are equal distance apart—such as the branch in Design 2, Part 19, or the vine in Design 1, stitch the concave (inside) curve FIRST. This becomes especially important when appliquéing the narrow bias of vines that loop and curl. If you stitch the convex (outside) curve first, the concave one tends to pucker, which is unattractive.

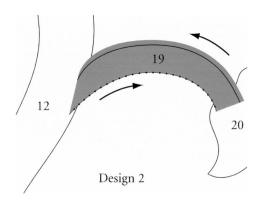

Concave and convex curves

"U" CURVES

Clip every ⅛" in the curve of the "U." Start stitching at the first clip.

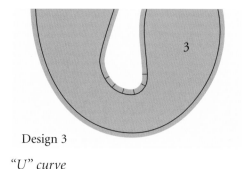

"U" curve

POINTS

1. Stitch to the marked point—not to the end of the fabric. Take another stitch on top of the last one to secure it.

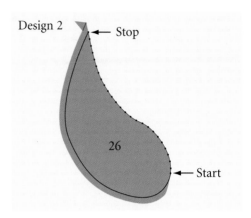

Point

2. Hold the stitch and the thread firmly under your thumbnail.
3. Turn the piece back on itself and trim away any excess seam allowance from the first side near the point.
4. With a quilter's pin (it's strong) grasp the ball between your thumb and index finger, braced from behind with your middle finger. Sweep the seam allowance under from right to left.
5. Then sweep it back from left to right, all the time holding the point tightly with your thumbnail, lifting it only when you sweep the fabric under. If you don't like the looks, pull it out with the pin and try again.
6. Don't let frays panic you. Consider them part of the seam allowance, which they are. Sweep them back under.
7. Still holding the point tightly, take a stitch into the background fabric about ¹⁄₁₆" out from the point. Unlike your other stitches you want this one to show. It will elongate the leaf, making it look even more pointed. After the piece is completely stitched, you can shape the point with your needle and press it with your thumbnail.

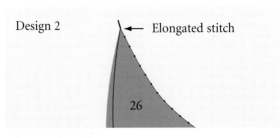

Elongated stitch

♪ *An elongated stitch is a show-off.*

CIRCLES

You want round round circles and you can have them if you mark them well, cut them well, and appliqué them well.

♪ *One stitch = secret to perfect circles.*

1. Use a pin on the underside to hold the circle piece in place.
2. Do not clip the seam allowance.
3. Needle turn for ONE stitch only.
4. Take that one stitch, turn the circle, then needle-turn again for one stitch only.
5. Take that stitch and turn the circle. Continue. Voila! A perfect circle with no puckers or points. (Example: Design 15, Part 4.)

DEEP "V's"

1. Clip the "V" to the marked line.
2. Stitch to the clip.
3. Flip under the loose side of the piece.
4. Take a stitch.
5. Flip it back. The seam allowance on the flipped part turns under by itself. Continue stitching.

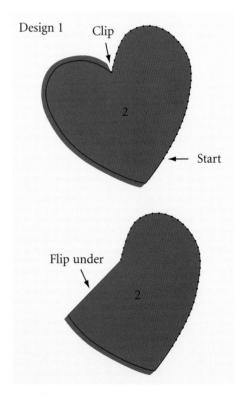

Deep "V"

SCALLOPS (SHALLOW "V's")

1. Clip at the "V."
2. Stitch to the clip.
3. Start needle turning at the next clip or 1½"–2" away from the last stitch on a big curve.
4. Needle turn in tiny increments BACK DOWN to the last stitch, maintaining the curve.
5. Take one stitch, yes, just one stitch.
6. Flip out the seam allowance that you've just turned under with your needle.
7. Proceed from the "V," needle turning enough for only ONE stitch.
8. Take that stitch and needle turn for the next stitch. Repeat.
9. Continue until you come to the next scallop.
10. Repeat steps 3-9.

Design 16

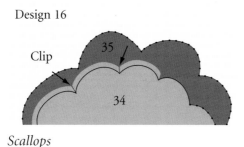

Scallops

TULIPS

The only templates provided are for the tulips found on pages 77 and 127.

1. For Design 3, lay the tulip cluster in its position on the background fabric.
2. Pin each piece, placing the pins on the WRONG side.
3. Remove the large piece (3); set aside.
4. Start stitching on the uppermost petal, flipping the others down out of your way. You don't need to stitch the part that goes under another piece. Continue with adjacent petals, one at a time, until all of the petals are stitched.
5. Lay the large piece (3) of the tulip in place.
6. You may choose to tuck a small contrasting piece of fabric under the "U" area.
7. Clip every ⅛" at the "U" on the inside bottom of the tulip. See the illustration for "U" curve, page 56.
8. Pin the side that has the STRAIGHT inside edge. Be sure to place pins on the back.

9. Pin the other side, overlapping the straight edge with the scalloped edge to cover where there is no seam allowance.
10. Start stitching where you first clipped. The slight pucker at the base will be eliminated when you stitch.

Design 3

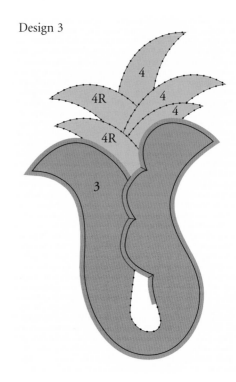

Tulip

The smaller tulip has no cluster. Start with step 6 (Design 21, Part 6).

BUTTING

When two pieces touch each other without overlapping, it's called "butting." The tendency to overlap or not to touch can be overcome.

1. Stitch the first piece down completely.
2. Pin the second piece in place.
3. About 1" from the contact point begin to stitch the second piece counter clockwise.
4. When you reach the contact point, join the two pieces with an elongated stitch as you did with the leaf points (page 57). This will ensure that the two pieces do butt.
5. Continue stitching to the place where you started.

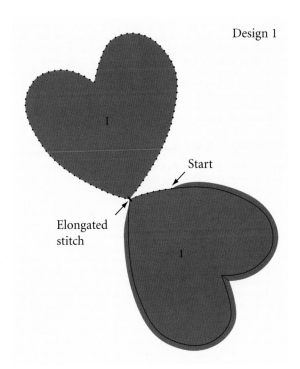

Design 1

Start

Elongated
stitch

HEAT BONDING (IRON-ON) METHOD

1. Trace around the plastic templates on the paper side of the fusible iron-on material. To duplicate the design positioning, turn the templates over. Right side up will reverse your design.
2. Cut on the line. No seam allowance is needed.
3. Place these on the WRONG side of the fabric you have chosen for the specific design pieces.
4. Follow the manufacturer's instructions for the recommended method of bonding. Be sure to pay attention to the temperature of your iron.

♪ *Heed the manufacturer.*

When you appliqué a border, whether by hand, machine, or iron-on technique, leave those pieces that cross a seam until after the top is assembled.

Butting

You may practice all of the techniques by appliquéing Designs 13 and 17.

MACHINE METHOD

There are a number of ways to machine appliqué. Satin stitch is the oldest and most common. You don't need a seam allowance, so you can cut the design piece along the line you have drawn around the template. A touch of spray adhesive will hold the piece in place while you're stitching. Use Sulky® or Metrosene thread. A short zigzag with close stitches, but not heavy, gives a nice appearance. Use your satin stitch foot or your buttonhole foot.

Try the "in" buttonhole stitch for a different look using Cordonnet thread. Invisible machine appliqué is very popular, with many books and classes available at quilt shops. If you don't know this technique, consider registering for a class.

ASSEMBLING THE QUILT

The score for each of the Jacobean Rhapsody quilts shows the cut and finished sizes of the blocks, border, sashing, and binding, and the finished size of the quilt. An illustration is provided for each of the Rhapsody quilts that shows the layout for each.

MITERING THE BORDER

All the Rhapsody quilts, but two, have mitered borders. *Rhapsody No. 6* has a pieced border and *Rhapsody No. 7* has a squared border (two long and two short pieces). Two Rhapsody quilts also have mitered sashing, and some have mitered bindings.

1. Cut the border the size indicated in the score.
2. Matching the midpoints of the border piece to the quilt top, pin the two together.
3. Sew with a ¼" seam, starting ¼" in from the edge of the quilt top and stopping ¼" from the other edge. Repeat for the other sides. Make certain the two seams meet at the corner.
4. Fold the quilt top, right sides together at the corners, so that the raw edges of the adjacent sides are even. Pin, and then turn the seams toward the quilt top. Pin the tails.
5. Lay the sides along a horizontal line on your cutting pad and lay the point where the two seams meet on the diagonal line that slants toward the tails.
6. Lay a ruler on the diagonal line, and draw a line from the inner corner to the raw edge of the pieces being mitered.
7. Start sewing at the inner corner and follow the line to the outer corner.
8. Finger press the diagonal seam open and the other seams toward the border. If the corner lies flat, trim the seam to ¼". If it does not lie flat, redo.

Sashings and bindings are made using the same method.

CUTTING THE BACKING

Be generous. Cut it larger than the quilt top so that it can be folded over to the front temporarily to protect the edges while you quilt.

QUILTING

You may have already made the decision whether to machine quilt or to hand quilt. Hand quilting is still in style. Its "look" is hard to compete with and it announces that the quiltmaker thought the work worthy of the time invested. Most of the Rhapsodies are hand quilted. However, machine quilting has come out of the wings and is having its turn in the spotlight. *Turkish Delight* by Pat Campbell and Michelle Jack, which won Best of Show at the 1997 Dallas Quilt Celebration, was machine quilted by Marcia Stevens, using Mettler thread. The machine quilting on *Rhapsody No.1* and *Rhapsody No. 2* by Randy Silvers is beautifully done. Use straight-line stitching, free-motion stitching, or a combination. Find the longest uninterrupted stitching path to minimize stopping and starting. If you haven't tried machine quilting, don't knock it. Remember the time saved means more time to appliqué. Refer to *Heirloom Machine Quilting* by Harriet Hargrave for more information on machine quilting.

Consider using metallic thread in combination with other thread for either hand or machine quilting. Outlining the designs, adding small crosshatching, meandering, or echo quilting are all effective.

QUILT SLEEVE

A wall quilt isn't finished until it has a sleeve for hanging. If you would like it to be of the same material as the backing, include it when figuring the amount of yardage needed.

A ¼" tuck on the sleeve side away from the quilt allows rod space, eliminating the quilt's tipping forward or the sleeve's showing at the top. The sleeve can be sewn on by machine with a ⅛" seam before binding or stitched by hand after binding.

BINDING

Now is the time to make some decisions about the binding: 1)the same fabric as the background or not? 2)what width? 3) single or double? 4) bias or straight grain? 5) sewn on before or after quilting? or 6) "false" or "true" mitered corners?

If you want the binding to be the same fabric, figure in the yardage when you decide on the background fabric. However, choosing one of the fabrics of your design pieces makes the binding a picture frame for your composition. A finished binding that is wider than ¾" is not advisable because it will overwhelm the design, especially for a small wall quilt. Consider using a ¼" binding for the Rhapsody quilts, although a ⅜" or a ½" binding may be used.

Some people like single binding and others like double binding. Originally double binding was used to make the quilt more durable. Quilts, you recall, were bedcovers and the man's beard would wear the edges as he tucked it under his chin for warmth. All ten quilts in this book are wall quilts, so a double binding isn't needed. For single binding, cut the width four times what you want the finished binding to be. Example: ¼" finished needs a 1" cut; ½", a 2" cut. For double binding, cut six times the finished width; for example, ¼" finished needs a 1½" cut; a ½" finished needs a 3" cut. Single is better for a ¼" binding.

Do use double, if you like the look, but only with straight grain strips. If you fold it in half lengthwise, then pin and sew the two raw edges together, it will be less likely to twist when being stitched on the quilt.

In the past, the binding was usually cut on the bias, perhaps because quilters didn't know how to turn the neat square corner that we do today. With bias, they could "round" the corners.

If you decide on a bias binding, be sure to cut true to the bias—the same width throughout and not even slightly off the 45° angle. The "tube" method for cutting bias is not recommended, because it's too easy to get off bias. A little at first adds up to a lot at the end. Follow the instructions for Cutting and Making Bias on page 54.

Hawaiians were making straight-grain binding while Mainlanders were still cutting bias binding. It's easy to measure for straight-grain binding: add 12" to the perimeter of your quilt. How much fabric is needed depends on how wide the strips are cut. If you're using the background fabric for binding, cut the two—background and binding—at the same time. Cut the strips as long as possible to minimize the number of joinings. Cut the ends of the strips on the diagonal, ready to join.

If you have a choice, cut lengthwise. Lengthwise cuts are more firm than crosswise cuts, and can help the outer border to remain straight. Do not mix them because the pieces will show the difference when they are sewn together. Sew and finger press the seams. Do not press the binding itself because there is a tendency, even for straight grain cuts, to stretch. You want to avoid waves.

Sometimes there's no choice but to cut the binding crosswise. To determine how much fabric you need, use the following formula: We will use *Rhapsody No.1* as the example.

1. Measure the perimeter of your quilt (64" x 4 = 256").
2. Add 12" (256" + 12" = 268").
3. Divide the result of Step 2 by 44" (the fabric width with the selvages removed). If it is a fraction, round it off to the next higher number (268"/44" = 7" widths, rounded up from 6.09).
4. Multiply the result of Step 3 by the width of the strip, and you will have the yardage needed (7 widths x 1" [¼" finished] = 7"). It is wise to purchase a ¼ yard.

Sewing the binding on "before quilting" permits you to be unencumbered by the batting and backing. If you prefer to stitch the binding on after quilting, you can protect the edge during quilting by turning the backing to the front and hand basting. If there is insufficient fabric to do this, hand baste muslin strips over the edge.

Either before or after quilting, start the procedure by squaring the top and then sewing on the binding, mitering the corners, and connecting the ends. If you quilt before binding, machine baste the three layers—top, batt, and backing—together ⅛" from the edge. This keeps the edges from flaring or shifting and lets you cut all three layers evenly. Trim the batt and backing even with the top.

MITERING THE BINDING

There are two methods for mitering the binding corners: the "true" miter, explained below, which can be done only with single binding, and the popular "false" miter, which can be done with either single or double binding.

The "false" miter and a simple method to connect the binding ends are very popular and can be found in a number of publications. We have explained this method in our previous books, *Jacobean Appliqué: Exotia* and *Jacobean Appliqué: Romantica*.

Use the finished width of the binding as the width of the seam allowance; for example, ¼" finished, ¼" seam allowance or ½" finished, ½" seam allowance. If binding is double, after sewing it to the quilt top, turn it to the wrong side of the quilt, pin and stitch. If single, turn it to the wrong side, folding it under so that the raw edge of the binding meets the raw edge of the quilt. Fold again, pin and stitch in place. The stitches can be ¼" apart rather than the ⅛" you used on the design pieces. When you come to the false miter, tack it down well, front and back. Judges will examine these corners; they will also check that the batt comes to the folded edge— that is it fills the binding.

The "true miter" and a ¼" finished binding width are recommended for *Rhapsody No.3* through *Rhapsody No.10*, because these wall quilts are small. By cutting the binding the full length of each side plus 3", you'll have no seams showing. On a large quilt these are not noticeable, but in a small one, the eye sees the whole at one time. Use only single thickness for this method. Double is too heavy at the corners and will not turn crisply.

1. After mitering the corners as you did with the borders (page 60), turn the quilt top to the wrong side. Fold the corner down on the diagonal, deep enough to produce a small square just below the sewing line that is the same size as the finished binding width (¼" square for ¼" finished binding). Cut away the square.

"True" mitering the binding

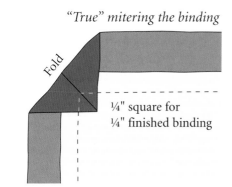

2. Fold down each side of the miter so that the raw edge of the binding and raw edge of the quilt meet.

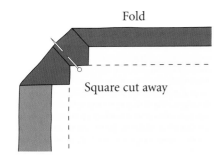

3. Fold down again, and pin.

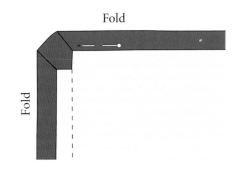

4. Stitch one fold along the seamline of the miter. Then stitch the other fold along the seamline of the miter. Repeat for the other three corners.

Fold

5. Fold and pin the rest of the binding in place, being careful to cover the sewing line.
6. Stitch in place, using a hidden appliqué technique with stitches ¼" apart.

COMPOSER

Use Pigma Micron® pens, which come in various colors, to write information either directly onto the back of your quilt or on a label to be attached to the back. Include the following: your name, the name of the quilt, the place it was made, the date, and any other information you would like present and future quilt lovers to know. Add your signature to all your projects as inconspicuously or as boldly as your ego prefers. Folks in the future will shout "bravo" when they discover you have provided such wonderful details.

If you prefer not to make a label by hand, try ironing freezer paper on the back of a piece of plain-colored fabric and then running it through your printer. Be sure the ink is completely dry before sewing it on your quilt.

APPLAUSE

Expect a standing ovation from friends and family when you show them the Rhapsody you have created. Although they may have heard a rhapsody, this will be the first time they've SEEN a Rhapsody.

♪ *Applause is a grace note.*

COMPOSE A JACOBEAN RHAPSODY

To help you compose your very own Rhapsody, these miniatures are proportionate, paired by size, and can be duplicated, cut apart, and then easily positioned in various combinations. Improvise! Rhapsodize!

5

8

21

18

11

24

4

17

10

6

7

3

23

19

20

16

Jacobean Rhapsodies

1

14

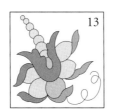

13

26

12

25

9

2

22

15

27

28

The authors and publisher give permission to photocopy a maximum
of two copies each of pages 64 to 65 for personal use only.

1-A

Design 1: Queen's Lace

Design 2:
𝒫rimrose 𝒯ree

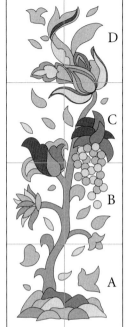

The authors and publisher give permission to photocopy a maximum
of two copies each of pages 69 to 72 for personal use only.

Design 3: Trumpet Tulips

3-A

The authors and publisher give permission to photocopy a maximum
of two copies each of pages 73 to 78 for personal use only.

3-D

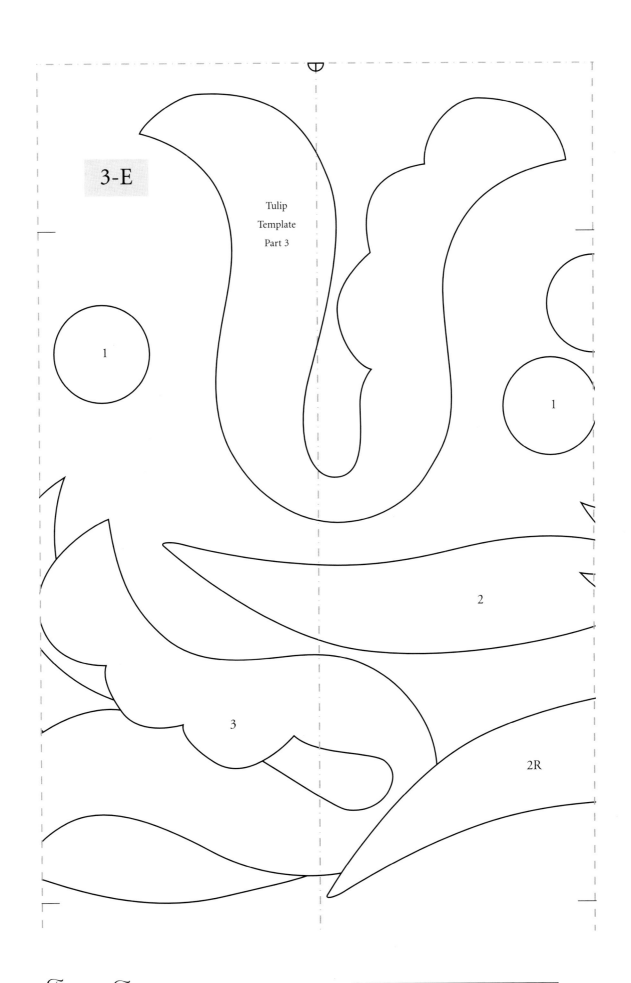

3-E

Tulip
Template
Part 3

1

1

2

3

2R

3-F

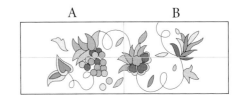

A   B

4-A

4-B

Design 5: Pixie Vine

5-A

5-B

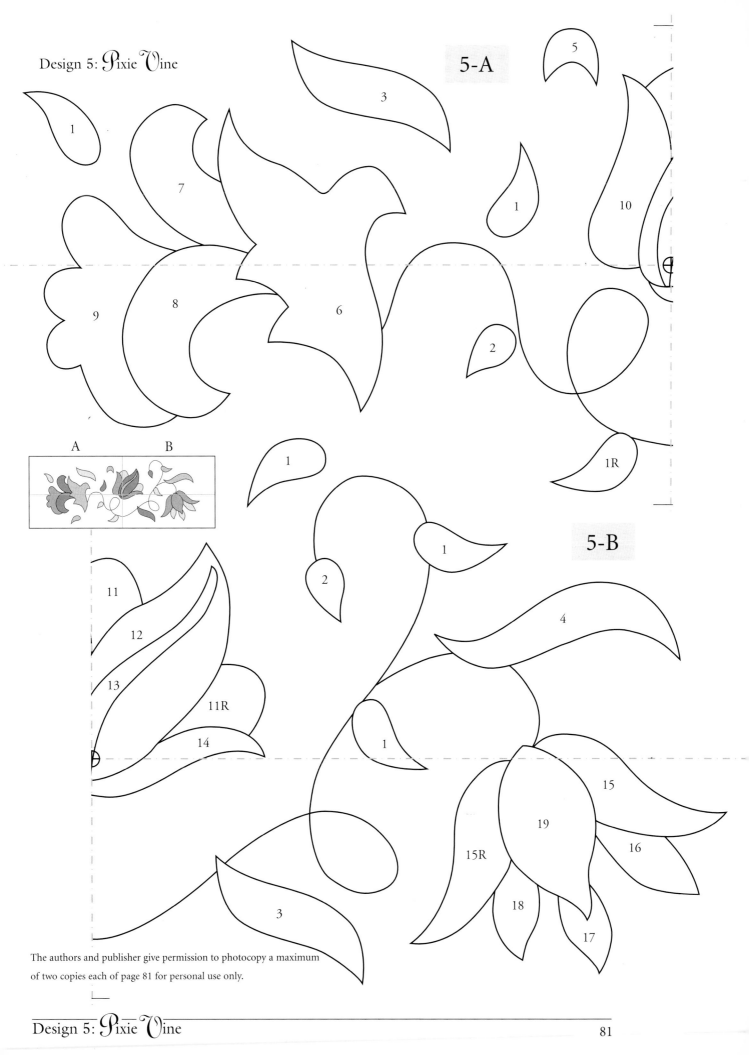

Design 6: Canterbury Bells

A B

6-A

17

16

29

31

30

28

22

8

21

14

13

15

12

C D

6-B

6-C

6-D

Design 7: Lancaster Oak Leaf

A   B

C   D

7-A

22

26R

26R

26R

25

28 27

24

23

20

21

26

26

26

17

16

12

14

A

7-C

7-D

34

15

9

8

7

3

4

3

Design 8: Oxford Oak

8-A

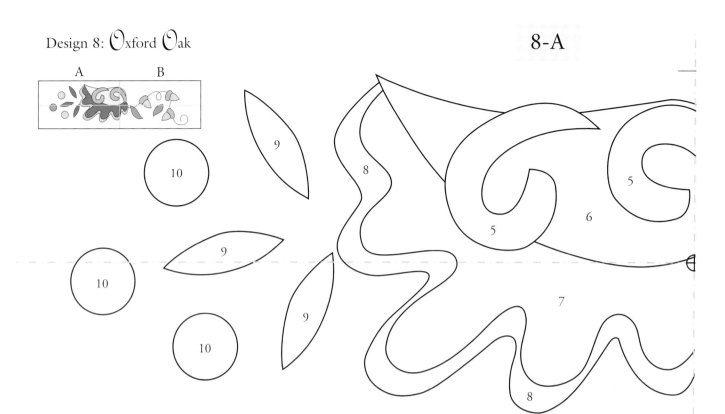

8-B

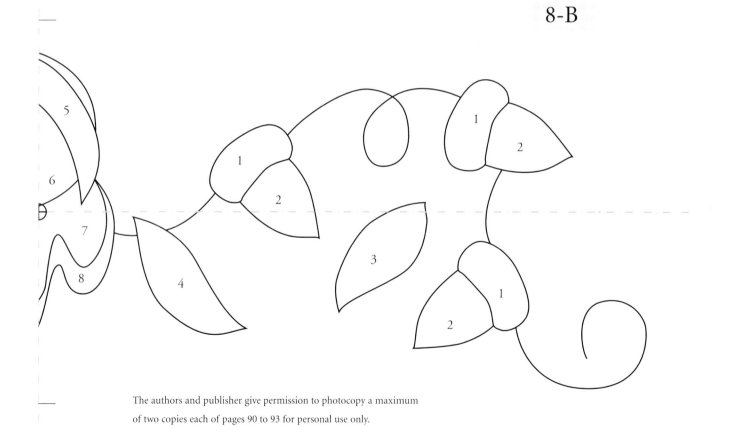

A
B
C

9-A

26

54

53

27

45

52

45

46

25

51

47

48

50

45

45R

49

45R

11

14

11

11

The authors and publisher give permission to photocopy a maximum
of two copies each of pages 91 to 93 for personal use only.

9-B

9-C

Design 10: Derby Swirl

10-A

A

B

1
1

29
28
27
25
24
26
23
21
21R
22
22R
20
2
4
18
19
17R
17
5
16
3

Jacobean Rhapsodies

10-B

Design 11: Chelsea Wattle

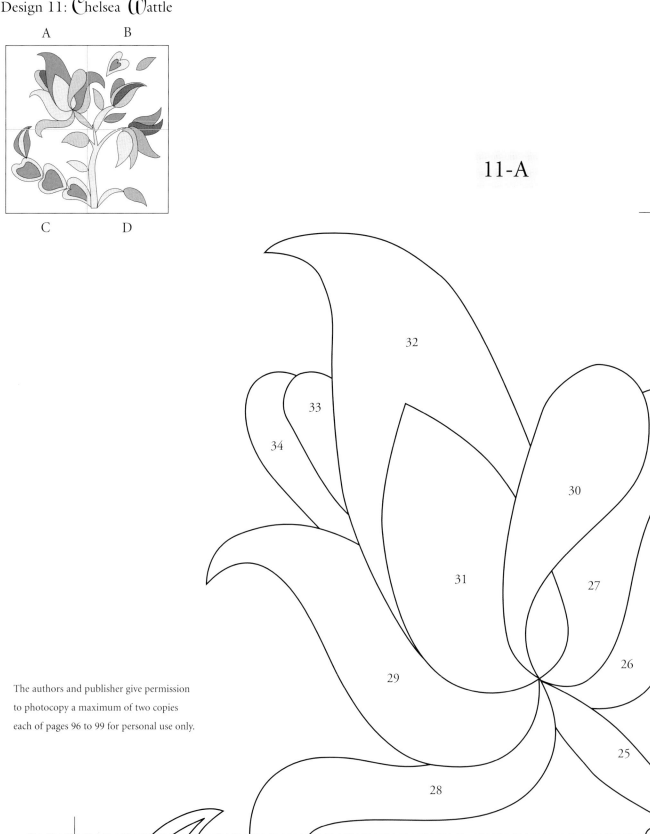

A   B

C   D

11-A

32

33

34

30

31

27

29

26

25

28

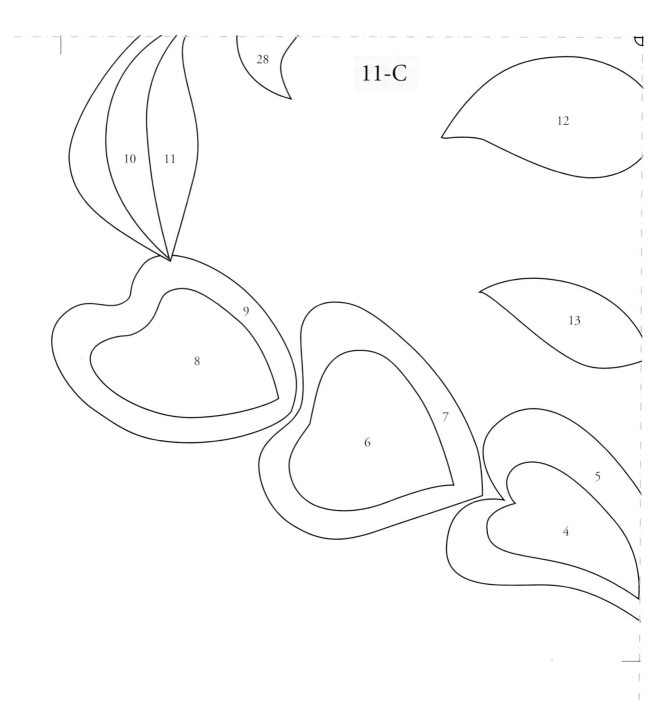

28

11-C

12

10 11

13

9

8

7

6

5

4

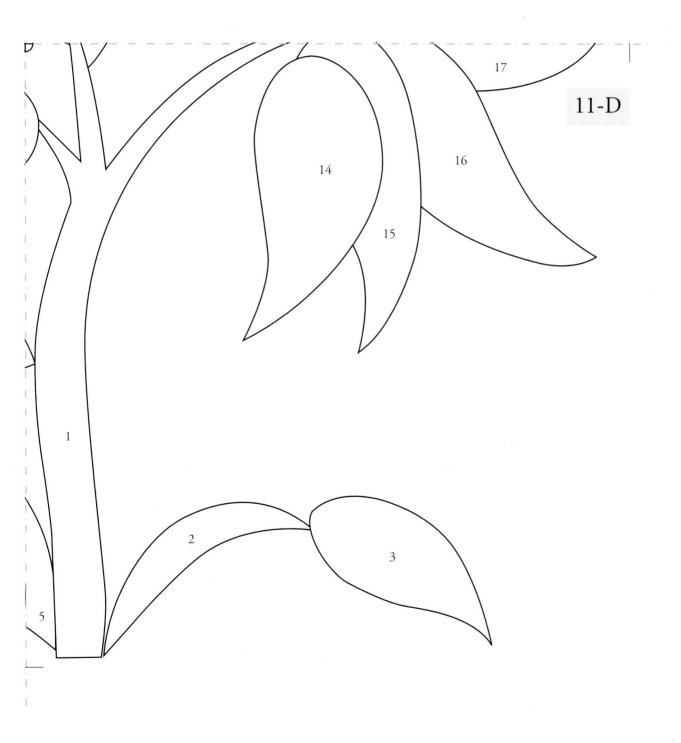

11-D

Design 12: Tulip Berry

12-A

Jacobean Rhapsodies

12-B

Design 12: Tulip Berry

Design 13: Tulip Swirl

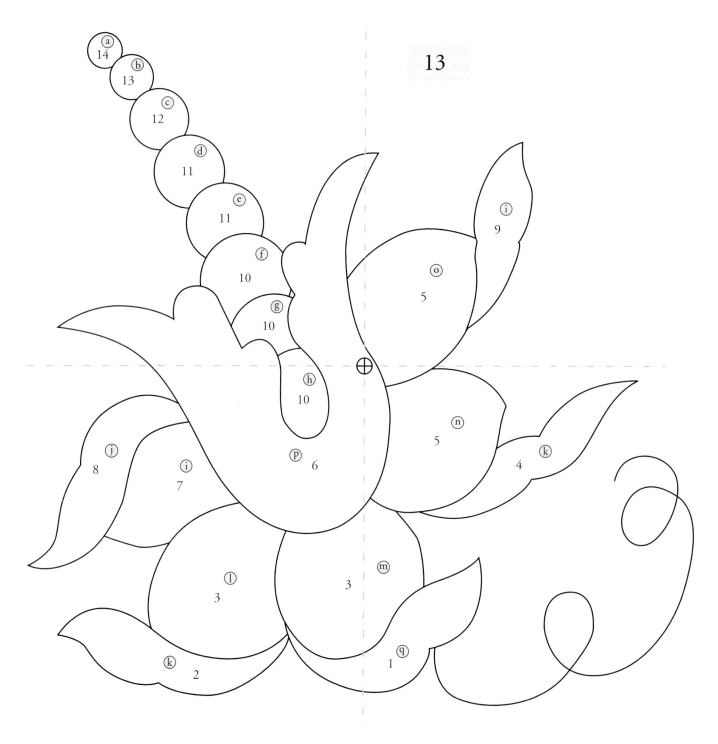

Design 14: Scarlet Cherry

A   B   C

14-A

13R

11

12

11R

12R

30

30

30

28

29

28R

27

10

10

10

25

6R

The authors and publisher give permission to photocopy a maximum
of two copies each of pages 103 to 105 for personal use only.

3

2

4

26

1

Design 15: Cambridge Vines

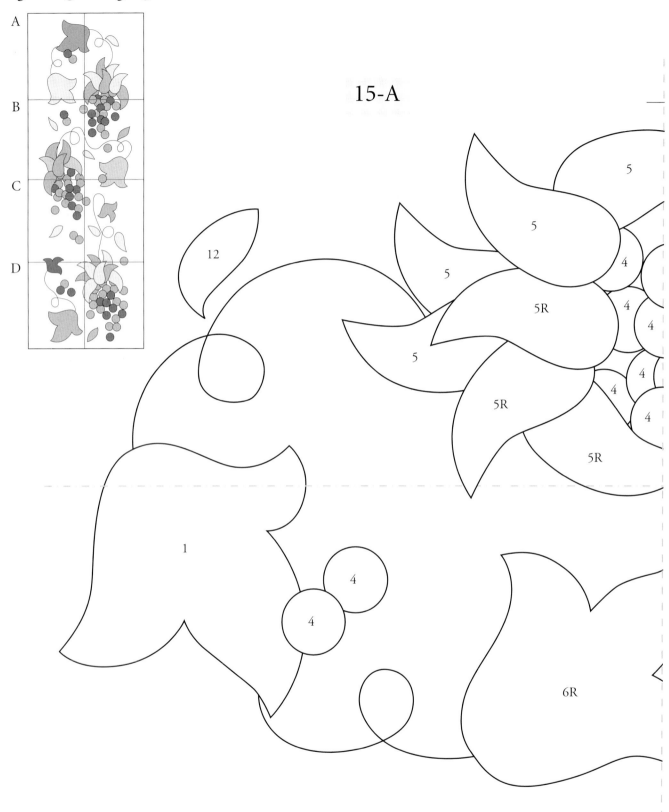

A
B
C
D

15-A

5

12

5

5

5R

5

5R

4

4

4

4

4

4

5R

1

4

4

6R

The authors and publisher give permission to photocopy a maximum
of two copies each of pages 106 to 109 for personal use only.

15-B

Design 15: Cambridge Vines

Jacobean Rhapsodies

Design 16: $\mathcal{W}$ind $\mathcal{T}$ree

16-A

A   B   C

D   E   F

10

53R

52R

48R

57R

50R

49

38

56

55

54

48

52

50

53

21

29

28

The authors and publisher give permission to photocopy a maximum

of two copies each of pages 110 to 115 for personal use only.

$\mathcal{J}$acobean $\mathcal{R}$hapsodies

16-B

16-D

16-E

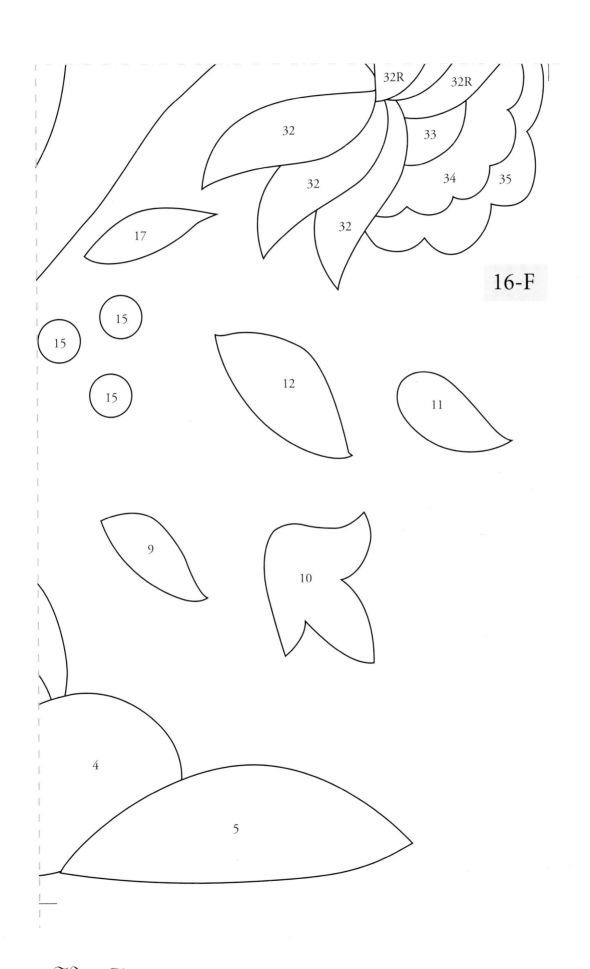

16-F

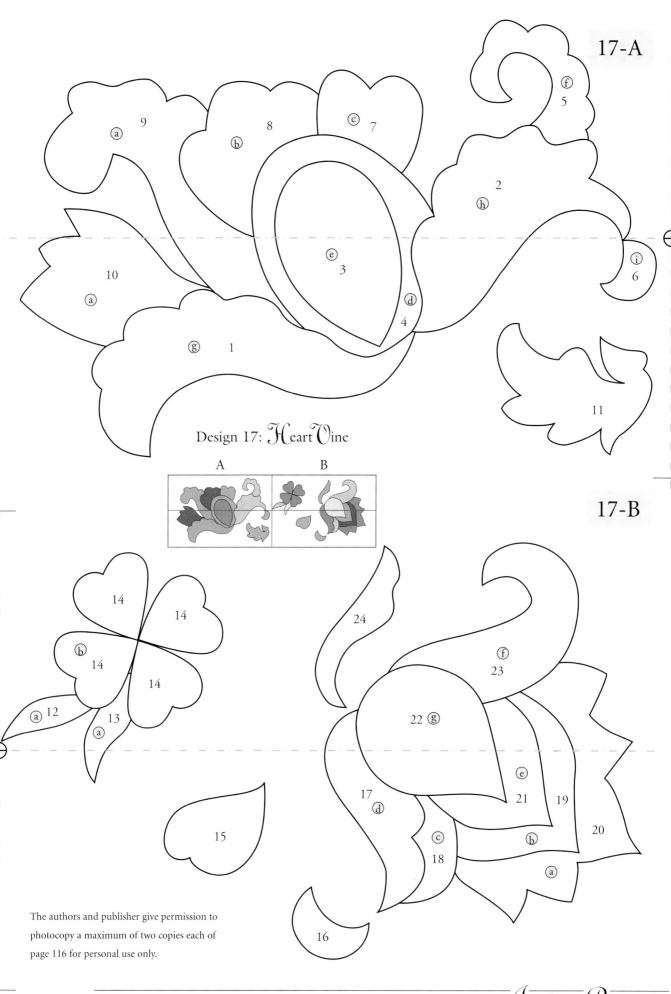

17-A

Design 17: $\mathcal{H}$eart $\mathcal{V}$ine

17-B

Design 18: Painted Hearts

A   B

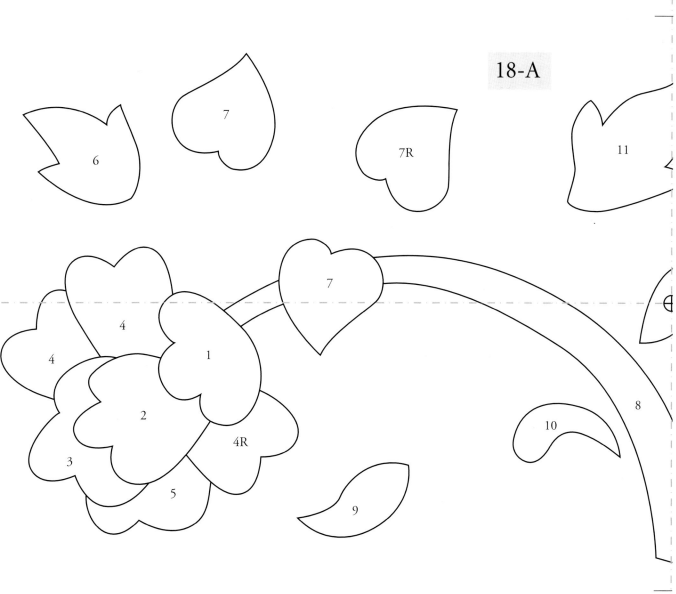

18-A

The authors and publisher give permission to photocopy a maximum
of two copies each of pages 117 to 118 for personal use only.

18-B

A   B

C   D

19-A

The authors and publisher give permission
to photocopy a maximum of two copies each
of pages 119 to 122 for personal use only.

52
52
53
52
52

21
15
52
51

Bias

14R
16
51

34
33

Bias

49 50
48
43
44
45
46
47

9

19-B

19-C

21R

23

22

24   23

23   21

16

Bias

33

15

54

Bias

13

12

11

17

9

10

8

55

7

1   2   3

19-D

Jacobean Rhapsodies

Design 20: Newcastle Vine

A   B

20-A

C   D

21R

Bias

20

1

22

2R

3

21

22

24

15

18

17

16

19

Bias

22

The authors and publisher give permission to photocopy a maximum
of two copies each of pages 123 to 126 for personal use only.

28

20-B

2

22

21R

21R

27

Bias

23

21

28

24

21

8

6

4

5

7

6

Bias

3

3

20-D

Design 21: $\mathcal{S}$weet $\mathcal{B}$riar

A   B

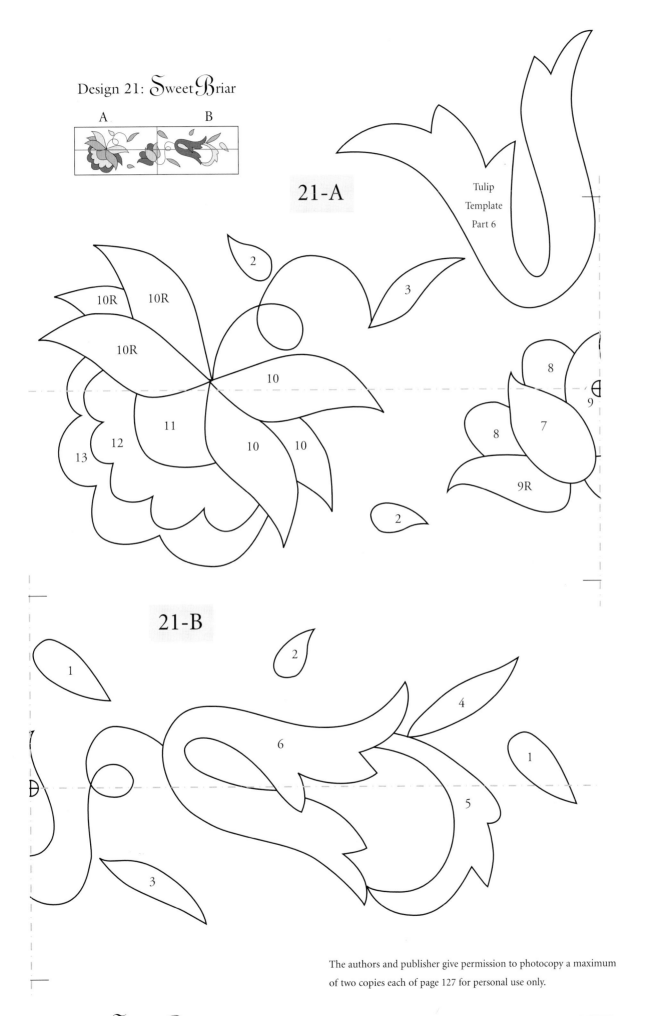

21-A

Tulip
Template
Part 6

2

10R   10R

10R

10

11

12

13   10   10

2

8

8   7

9

9R

21-B

1

2

4

6

1

5

3

The authors and publisher give permission to photocopy a maximum
of two copies each of page 127 for personal use only.

Design 22: Windsor Sunflower

A

B

C

22-A

36

29

34

33

35

32

33

9

28

34

8

20

31

30

1

21

19

17

1

19

1

17

27R

Jacobean Rhapsodies

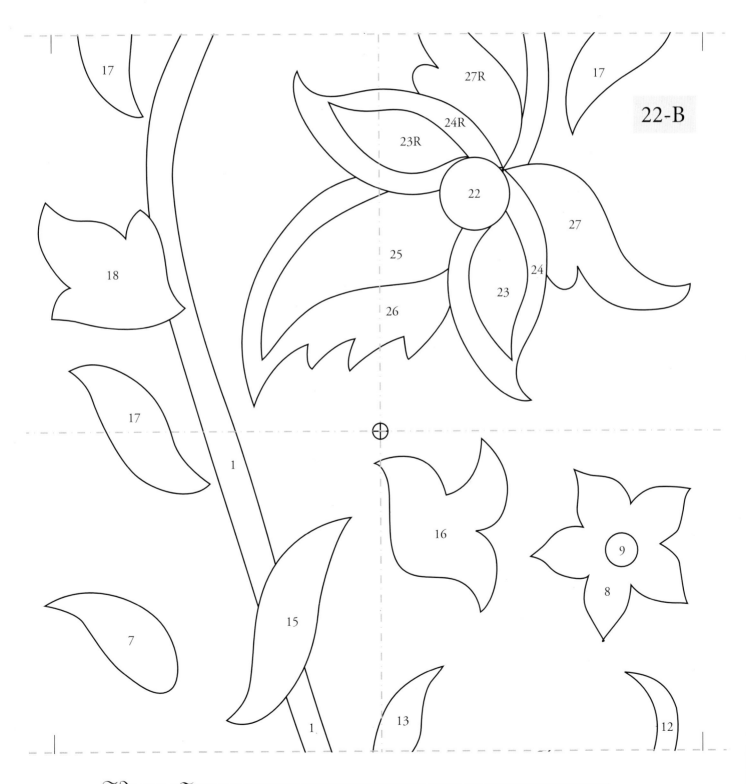

22-C

Design 23: Passion Vine

A

B

The authors and publisher give permission
to photocopy a maximum of two copies each
of pages 131 to 132 for personal use only.

Bias

23-B

Design 24: $\mathcal{L}$ancaster $\mathcal{T}$ulip

24-A

24-B

24-C

Design 25: Silky Oak

A

B

25-A

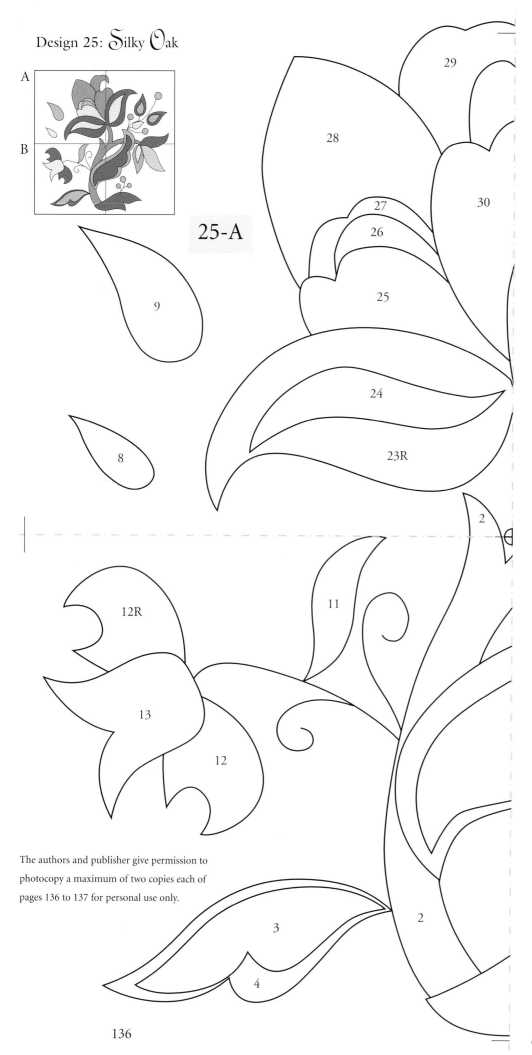

9

8

28

29

30

27

26

25

24

23R

2

12R

11

13

12

The authors and publisher give permission to
photocopy a maximum of two copies each of
pages 136 to 137 for personal use only.

3

2

4

Design 25: Silky Oak

Design 26: Fairy Apron

12

12R

12R

12R

77

12

26

27

12R

12

12R

12R

11

12R

15R

76

Design 27: Queen's Garden

A   B   C

Design 27: Queen's Garden

D   E   F

27

26

75R

119

118

117

120

30

112

115

116

114

113

15

Design 27:
Queen's Garden

G   H

3

2

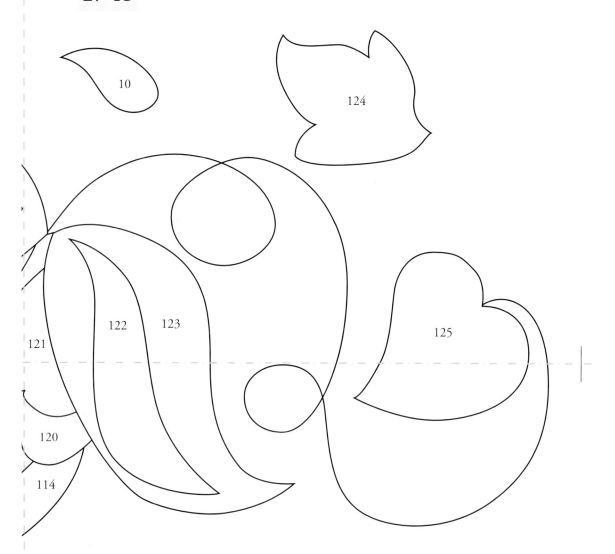

10

124

122 123

121

125

120

114

15

28-A

72

73

74

71

69R

70

69

69

67+

67+

68

67+

67+

75

67+

67+

Design 28: Queen's Garden

A   B   C

The authors and publisher give permission to photocopy
a maximum of two copies each of pages 147 to 155 for
personal use only.
The + indicates pieces to be appliquéd after mitering.

28-B

29

63

62

59

58

60

61

10R

57

62R

11R

Design 28: Queen's Garden

50

27

26

9

42

30

44R

44R

44

44R

45

47

46

45

43

48

46

44

44

49

Design 28: Queen's Garden

D   E   F

28-F

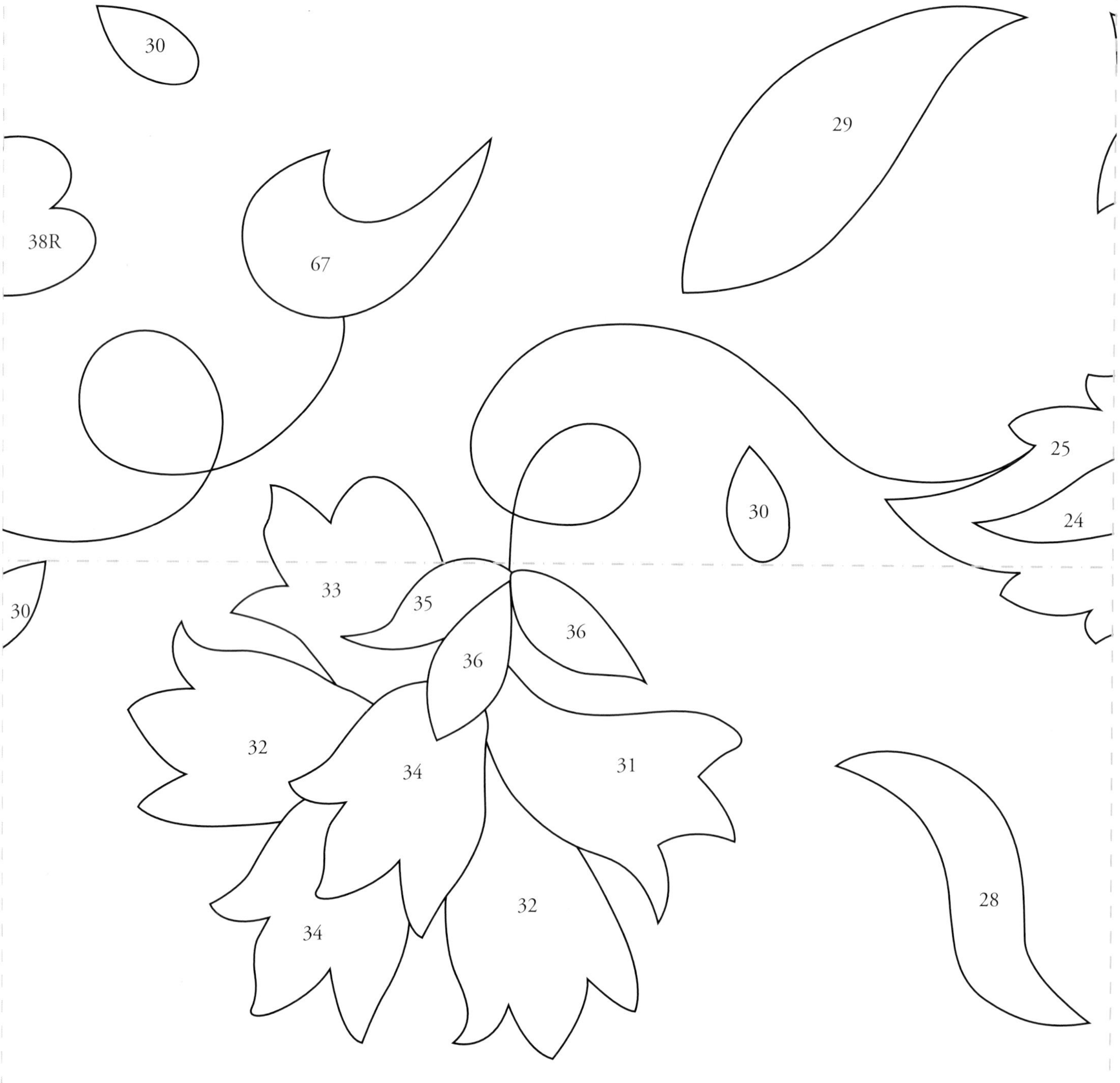

30
29
38R
67
25
30
24
30
33
35
36
36
32
34
31
28
34
32

28-G

27

26

29

15

25

17

15

24

18

19

20

17

21

22

16

14

23

Design 28: Queen's Garden

G   H   I

Design 28: Queen's Garden   153

28-H

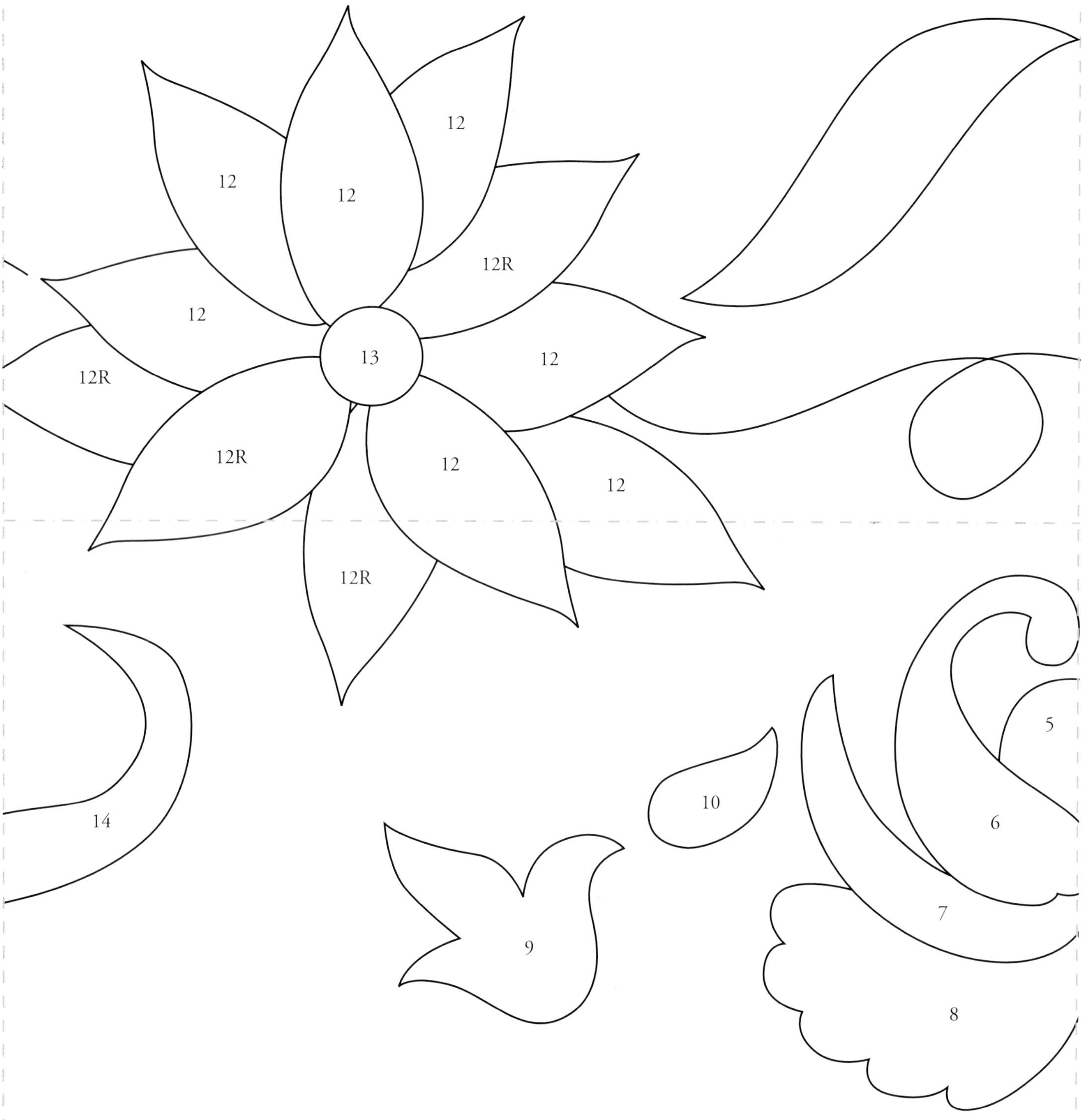
12
12
12
12R
12
13
12
12R
12R
12
12
12R
5
14
10
6
9
7
8

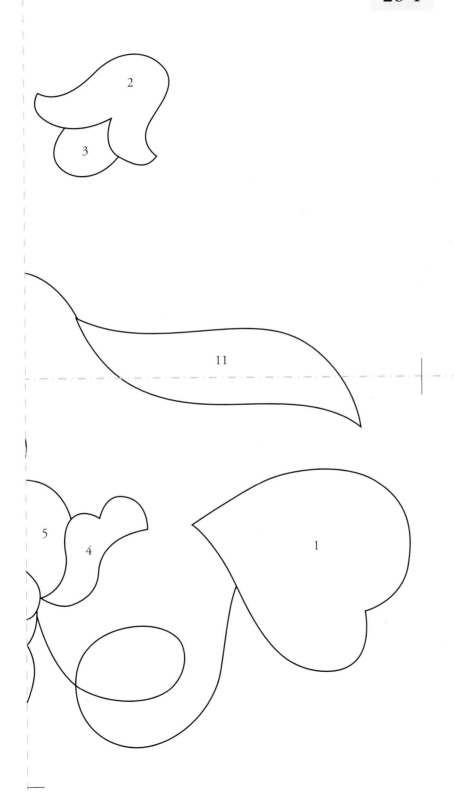

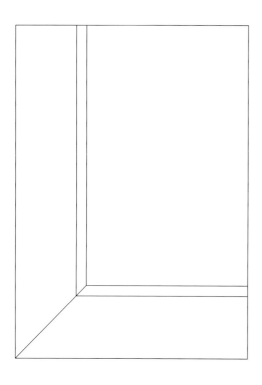

The Score for J A C O B E A N   R H A P S O D Y   N O .   3

QUILT   23" x 32"
BINDING   ¼" wide, finished
DESIGN   Variations of 1, 10, 14, and 19

	Cut Size*	Finished Size
BLOCK	17" x 26"	16" x 25"
SASHING	one 1 ½" x 19"	1" x 17"
	one 1 ½" x 28"	1" x 26"
BORDER	one 7" x 25"	6" x 23"
	one 7" x 34"	6" x 32"

After the block is appliquéd, add a ¼" seam allowance to all four sides of the Finished Size, then trim the extra fabric from the edges.
Trim the width of the border after appliquéing and trim the ends after mitering.

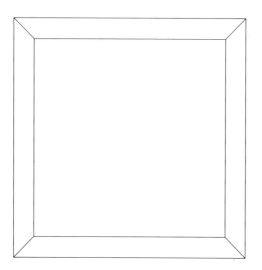

The Score for J A C O B E A N   R H A P S O D Y   N O .   4

QUILT   23" x 23"
BINDING   ¼" wide, finished
DESIGN   3 — *a coin (a quarter) makes a good template for Part 1*

	Cut Size*	Finished Size
BLOCK	20" x 20"	19" x 19"
BORDER	four 2 ½" x 27"	2" x 23"

After the block is appliquéd, add a ¼" seam allowance to all four sides of the Finished Size, then trim the extra fabric from the edges.

The Score for J A C O B E A N   R H A P S O D Y   N O. 5

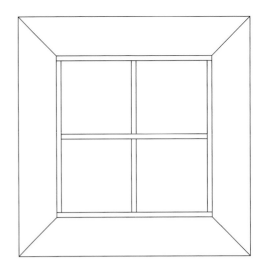

	Cut Size*	Finished Size
QUILT	49" x 49"	
BINDING	¼" wide, finished	
DESIGNS	11, 12, 24, 25, and variations of these designs for the border	

	Cut Size*	Finished Size
BLOCKS	16" x 16"	15" x 15"
BORDER	four 9" x 53"	four 8" x 49"
SASHING	two 1 ½" x 15 ½"	two 1" x 15"
	three 1 ½" x 31 ½"	three 1" x 31"
	two 1 ½" x 33 ½"	two 1" x 33"

After the block is appliquéd, add a ¼" seam allowance to all four sides of the Finished Size, then trim the extra fabric from the edges.
Trim the width of the border after appliquéing and trim the ends after mitering.

The Score for J A C O B E A N   R H A P S O D Y   N O. 6

QUILT	20" x 34"	
BINDING	¼" wide, finished	
DESIGN	9	

	Cut Size	Finished Size
BLOCK	13" x 27"	12" x 26"
BORDER	two rows of 2" quarter-square triangles	four 4" wide, pieced

After the block is appliquéd, add a ¼" seam allowance to all four sides of the Finished Size, then trim the extra fabric from the edges.

Cut forty-six 3 ¼" light squares

and forty-six 3 ¼" dark squares.

Cut on the diagonal, twice.

Sew together for

ninety-two 2" finished blocks.

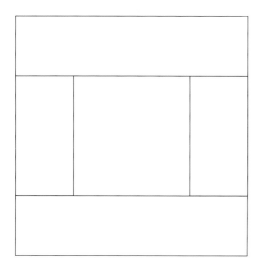

The Score for J A C O B E A N   R H A P S O D Y   N O .   7

QUILT   32" x 32"
BINDING   ⅜" wide, finished
DESIGNS   Variations of 4, 23, 26

	Cut Size*	Finished Size
BLOCK	17" x 17"	16" x 16"
SIDE BORDER	two 9" x 17"	two 8" x 16"
TOP/BOTTOM BORDER	two 9" x 33"	two 8" x 32"

*After the block is appliquéd, add a ¼" seam allowance to all four sides of the Finished Size, then trim the extra fabric from the edges.

*Trim the borders after appliquéing so they measure the Finished Size plus the ¼" seam allowances on all four sides.

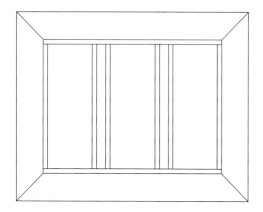

The Score for J A C O B E A N   R H A P S O D Y   N O .   8

QUILT   50" x 39 ½"
BINDING   ⅜" wide, finished
DESIGNS   Variations of 2, 9, 22

	Cut Size *	Finished Size
BLOCKS	three 11 ½" x 28"	10 ½" x 27"
BORDER	two 6 ¼" x 54"	5 ¾" x 50"
	two 6 ¼" x 43"	5 ¾" x 39 ½"
PANEL DIVIDERS	two 2 ½" x 27 ½"	2" x 27"
SASHING	six 1" x 27 ½"	½" x 27"
	two 1" x 39"	½" x 38 ½"

*After the block is appliquéd, add a ¼" seam allowance to all four sides of the Finished Size, then trim the extra fabric from the edges.

Jacobean Rhapsodies

The Score for J A C O B E A N   R H A P S O D Y   N O . 9

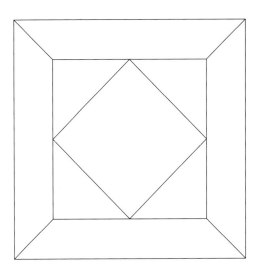

QUILT   42" x 42"
BINDING   ½" wide, finished
DESIGNS   16, 23

	Cut Size*	Finished Size
DESIGN BLOCK	20 ½" x 20 ½"	one 19 ½" x 19 ½"
CORNER BLOCKS	two 14 ⅞" squares,	four half-square traingles
	cut in half diagonally	14" x 14" x 19 ½"
BORDER	four 8" x 46"	four 7" x 42"

*After the block is appliquéd, add a ¼" seam allowance to all four sides of the Finished Size, then trim the extra fabric from the edges.

*Trim the width of the border after appliquéing and trim the ends after mitering.

The Score for J A C O B E A N   R H A P S O D Y   N O . 10

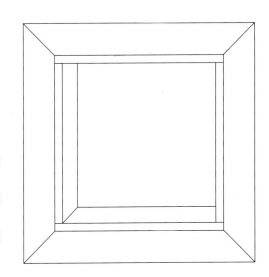

QUILT   30" x 30
BINDING   ¼" wide, finished
DESIGN   16

	Cut Size*	Finished Size
BLOCK	19" x 19"	18" x 18"
1st BORDER	two 2 ½" x 22"	two 2" x 20"
2nd BORDER	two 1 ½" x 20 ½"	two 1" x 20"
	two 1 ½" x 22 ½"	two 1" x 22"
3rd BORDER	four 4 ½" x 34"	four 4" x 30"

*After the block is appliquéd, add a ¼" seam allowance to all four sides of the Finished Size, then trim the extra fabric from the edges.

INDEX

appliqué
  hand, 52, 54
  Jacobean, def, 5
  machine, 52, 59

backing, 60
basting, 54
batting, 51
bell pull, 47
bias
  cutting, 54
  making, 49, 54
  press bar, 49
  binding, 60-62
bonding, heat, 52, 59
butting, 58

circles, 57
crewel work, 5
curves
  convex, 56
  concave, 56
  U, 56

designs
  design 1, 6, 36, 66
  variation, 38, 156
  design 2, 7, 36, 69
  variation, 43, 158
  design 3, 8, 36, 39, 73, 156
  design 4, 9, 36, 79
  variation, 42, 158
  design 5, 10, 36, 46, 47, 81
  design 6, 11, 36, 82
  design 7, 12, 36, 46, 86
  design 8, 13, 36, 90
  design 9, 14, 36, 41, 91, 157
  variation, 43, 158
  design 10, 15, 36, 94
  variation, 156
  design 11, 16, 36, 40, 96, 157
  design 12, 17, 36, 40, 100, 157
  design 13, 18, 33, 36, 47, 102
  design 14, 19, 37, 103
  variation, 38, 156
  design 15, 20, 37, 47, 106
  design 16, 21, 37, 44, 45, 46, 110, 159

design 17, 22, 33, 37, 116
design 18, 23, 37, 117
design 19, 24, 37, 119
variation, 38, 156
design 20, 25, 37, 123
design 21, 26, 37, 47, 127
design 22, 27, 37, 128
variation, 43, 158
design 23, 28, 37, 44, 131, 159
variation, 42, 158
design 24, 29, 37, 40, 133, 157
design 25, 30, 37, 40, 47, 136, 157
design 26, 31, 37, 138
variation, 42, 158
design 27, 32, 37, 46, 139
variation, 40, 157
design 28, 32, 37, 147
variation, 40, 157

emery board, 49
eraser, 49

fabric
  color, 50
  cutting, 52
  marking, 52
  not marking, 54
  type, 50
Fran's Quilt Shop, 4

glasses, 48

hosiery case, 47

jacket, 46
Jacobean
  appliqué (def), 5
  embroidery, 5, 33
jumper, 46

label, 63
lamp, 48
lightbox, 49

magnet, 48
mitering, 60-62

needles, 48

panels, 49
pattern, master
  material, 51
  making, 52
pencils, 48
pens, 49
photo album cover, 47
pin cushion, 48
pins, 48
placemats, 47
points, 57

quilts
  Jacobean Rhapsody No. 1, 2, 4, 33, 34, 36
  Jacobean Rhapsody No. 2, 2, 4, 33, 35, 37
  Jacobean Rhapsody No. 3, 2, 38, 54, 62, 156
  Jacobean Rhapsody No. 4, 39, 156
  Jacobean Rhapsody No. 5, 40, 157
  Jacobean Rhapsody No. 6, 41, 60, 157
  Jacobean Rhapsody No. 7, 42, 54, 60, 158
  Jacobean Rhapsody No. 8, 43, 158
  Jacobean Rhapsody No. 9, 44, 159
  Jacobean Rhapsody No. 10, 45, 62, 159

quilt sleeve, 60
quilting, 60

rhapsody, musical 5
Rule of the Triangle, 51

sandpaper board, 48
scallops, 58
scissors, 48
skirt, 46
stitchers
  Anderson, Beth C., 45, 46
  Anderson, Kathleen, 47
  Anderson, Virginia, 11
  Bird, Sheila, 10, 46
  Cadwallender, Deborah L., 7

Caterino, Martha, 8
Chambers, Sharon, 43
Cook, Janice L., 27
Dupré, Alexandra Capadalis, 47
Edwards, Florence, 22
Foote, Betty, 14, 42
Fox, C. Louise, 16
Gammell, Judy, 24
Golub, Mitzi, 47
Haese, Vanessa, 21
Hamrin, Barbara, 32
Hill, Sara P., 15
Hodge, Rhonda Bellamy, 46
Johnson, Verona R., 13
McArthur-Engle, Jamie, 47
McCabe, Jane, 6, 40
McCabe, Pam, 28
McCourt, Ann, 12
McLean, Michelle, 29, 41
Oravetz, Jane (Walters), 17
Rapa, Laura, 38
Ribbett, Bea, 39
Sargent, Latricia, 26
Schlactus, Kristen, 18, 31
Silvers, Randy, 4
Sutton, Carole, 25
Van Nest, Lynn M., 30, 38
Vieaux, Geraldine A., 20, 44
Wagner, Judy, 9
Wheatley, Mary E., 32
Willett, Terri, 19
Woodward, Sharon, 45
Young, Betty, 45
Zeida, Debra Botelho, 23

T-square, 49
template
  circle, 49
  material, 51
thimble, 48
thread, 51
tote, 47
tulips, 58

V's, 57
vest, 47

Web of Thread, 47
wine sack, 47

BIBLIOGRAPHY

Campbell, Patricia and Ayars, Mimi, *Jacobean Appliqué, Book I Exotica* (Paducah, AQS, 1993).

_____. *Jacobean Appliqué, Book II Romantica* (Paducah, AQS, 1995).

Hargrave, Harriet, *From Fiber to Fabric*, (Lafayette, C&T Publishing, Inc., 1997)

For more information, write for a free catalog to:
C&T Publishing, Inc.
P.O. Box 1456, Lafayette, CA 94549
(800)284-1114
http://www.ctpub.com
e-mail:ctinfo@ctpub.com

For quilting supplies:
Cotton Patch Mail Order
3405 Hall Lane, Dept. CTB, Lafayette, CA 94549
e-mail quiltusa@yahoo.com
Web:www.quiltusa.com
(800) 835-4418
(925) 283-7883